TRiZOPHRENiA

TRIZOPHRENIA

Inside the Minds of a Triathlete

Written and
Illustrated by
JEF MALLETT

BOULDER, COLORADO

1830 55th Street
Boulder, Colorado 80301-2700 USA
303/440-0601 · Fax 303/444-6788 · E-mail velopress@competitorgroup.com

Distributed in the United States and Canada by Ingram Publisher Services

Library of Congress Cataloging-in-Publication Data
Mallett, Jef
Trizophrenia: inside the minds of a triathlete / Jef Mallett.
        p. cm.
ISBN 978-1-934030-44-8 (pbk.: alk. paper)
1. Triathlon. 2. Sports—Psychological aspects. I. Title.
GV1060.73.M35 2009
796.42'57—dc22
                        2009037499

For information on purchasing VeloPress books, please call 800/234-8356 or visit www.velopress.com.

Cover and interior design by Erin Johnson

09   10   11 / 10   9   8   7   6   5   4   3   2   1

To all the athletes and writers and thinkers who have left me in the dust. If I can't stand on the shoulders of giants, maybe I can draft off them.

CONTENTS

Foreword by Peter Sagal. ix

Introduction: The Power of Three   **1**

PART I: WHAT IT IS

1. The Structure of a Sport with a Simple Structure   **9**
One: The swim 11
Two: The bike. 17
Three: The run. 23

2. A Brief History of a Sport with a Brief History   **29**
One: When it started 31
Two: How it started. 36
Three: Why it stuck. 41

3. Your Future in a Sport You Can Do for the Rest of Your Life   **47**
One: What to do. 49
Two: What to expect. 53
Three: How to explain it. 58

PART II: WHAT IT'S LIKE

1. Training Day   **69**
One: The time. 71
Two: The effort 76
Three: The economics. 84

2. Rest Day   **95**
One: Gosh, you look great. 97
Two: Gosh, you feel great. 102
Three: Gosh, you're cranky, irritable, and impossible to live with. . . 107

3. The Race   **113**
One: The race preparation. 115
Two: The race. 121
Three: The vibe 128

PART III: WHAT IT TAKES

1. What We've Learned About Our Resources   137
One: The money 139
Two: The smarts 144
Three: The discipline. 149

2. What We've Learned About Our Bodies   155
One: Fuel. 157
Two: Durability 163
Three: Talents 168

3. What We've Learned About Our Heads   173
One: Guts 175
Two: Determination. 180
Three: Appetite 185

Epilogue   191

Appendix by Patty Mallett 193
Acknowledgments. 197
About the Author and Illustrator. 199

FOREWORD

MY UNDERSTANDING OF THE CONVENTION of foreword writing—I've never written one before—is that one tends to be vague about the date on which said foreword was written, so as to create a timeless welcome to the tome that follows. Whenever you picked up this book, be it fresh off the "new arrivals" table or fished out of the remainders bin (sorry, Jef)—or perhaps, thirty years from now, as an assigned text in your Classic Contemporary Athletic Nonfiction class at Harvard (does that make up for the remainders bin, Jef?)—I would be here, in my avatar of print, welcoming you to the book, pointing, if you will, *foreword* to the experience at hand.

Not this time. I'm telling you flat out: I'm writing this on August 16, 2009.[1] Anything that's happened after that date, I don't know anything about, and may never know.[2]

Jef Mallett (who, as of this writing,[3] I have never met in person or even spoken to on the phone) and I have a lot in common. To wit: we are both forty-something married humorists living in the Midwest and are both obsessive/evangelical about endurance sports, in which we have been engaging, off and on, since our adolescence. We are also exactly the same modest height, 5 foot 7 inches, though I am somewhat thicker through the chest than he.[4] And we both have an enduring, if annoying, love of footnotes.

Here's where we differ: First, he's a talented cartoonist, known for his editorial work and his syndicated strip, *Frazz*, the most artfully drawn newspaper comic since Bill Watterson gave it all up to go illustrate J. D. Salinger's latest novel, whereas I can't draw a stick figure without observers wondering what horrible bone disease has afflicted the poor fellow. Second, he has to be funny every day, and generally succeeds, whereas I have to be funny but once a week and insist on applying the "if you fail two out of every three times, you're an All Star" standard of professional baseball. Last, and most important, he is a triathlete, and I am not. Yet.[5]

---

1   Tell you why in a minute.
2   You'll see what I mean in a minute.
3   See note 1.
4   Tell you how I know in a moment.
5   We're getting there.

I am a *runner*, a sweaty, annoyingly obsessed, hard-core runner, although I haven't always been. I started life as a pudgy little specimen of *Homo sapiens dorkimus*, my nose in books and my hand holding a fork or ice-cream cone, mindlessly eating and reading and eating some more and avoiding anything that even smelled like athletics because I was bad at it and had learned that failure was humiliating and stinging and bitter, and it was far, far better simply to avoid the attempt. Quitters never win, it's true, but the secret cherished by the nonparticipant is that quitters also never lose because we decided to sit out the race and go reread *The Lord of the Rings* while eating Nutella straight from the jar.

Okay, this is not precisely true. Sometimes quitters lose because the goddamn authority figures in our life wouldn't let us quit. Viz., the most humiliating experience in my pubescent life, the All-School Boys' Wrestling Tournament at Columbia Junior High School, Berkeley Heights, New Jersey, in the spring of 1979. One of the gym teachers, whose name I have mercifully forgotten but whose reddish Afro[6] and handlebar mustache haunt my nightmares to this day, loved wrestling and thus created the Wrestling Unit, in which all boys had to (1) learn to wrestle and then (2) compete against each other, climaxing in a tournament, with matches between the two finalists in each weight class, in front of the whole school at an annual assembly. The prior year, as a fat and slow seventh grader, I had been able to get out of it somehow, and I'd spent the four weeks playing volleyball or softball or tiddlywinks or whatever those benighted phys. ed. teachers in that benighted time reserved for girls and the infirm, but by the eighth grade even I, who had spent my youth gladly choosing the minor humiliation in the hand rather than the two major ones waiting in the bush, had no other option: I had to wrestle.

I went through the drills and the lessons, doing my pathetic best, comfortable in the knowledge that anyone with my poor skills and flabby physique would never get within smelling distance of the finals. We had one practice match before the preliminary rounds began, and, surprisingly, I won because my opponent, Robert Steingas,[7] suddenly folded up on me and I was able to pin him. Turned out, as he explained in gasps to me later, I had kneed him in the groin. By accident, honest. Then the Afro gave me some horrible news with a malicious grin. In the entire eighth grade, there were two, and only two, boys in the 135-pound weight class: Bruce Bennett[8] and me. Most of my 135 pounds were accumulated

---

6   What do you call one of those 1970s-era 'fros if the wearer was white? "Jewfro" does not apply, as he was not one of that tribe. "Caucfro"?

7   His real name.

8   Also his real name. Hey, Bruce!

Nutella. Bruce's were muscle. Nonetheless, we were automatically finalists, and thus we would be having our one and only match in the tournament, for the weight class title, in front of the whole school, a week hence.

A smarter boy would have prepared and practiced. A more practical boy would have fled. I just worried, and dreaded, and tried to pretend it wasn't happening—until the day it happened: me, standing on the mat opposite Bruce Bennett, in front of three hundred screaming, yelling, and cheering adolescents, many of them *girls*. I felt, naturally, terror, but also a kind of wonderment and thrill: I had never done anything like this. Maybe I would surprise myself. Maybe I would reveal something of myself, to myself and to the world at large, shocking all and thrilling some. I remember that moment vividly.

But not as vividly as the moment that soon followed, when the whistle blew and I started to think about perhaps moving to the right, or maybe to the left, and Bruce Bennett hit me like a milk truck and I flew backward, his arms grabbing mine, and I bounced once or twice, cushioned by Nutella, struggled a tad, and then relaxed into the warm embrace of the inevitable, and the final whistle, and the Afro's announcement: "Winner by a pin in eight seconds . . ."—a school record that still stands, I imagine—and the laughter, much of it girlish, drowning all. I laughed, too, of course. I laughed and laughed and laughed.

I stopped pretending to find it all so droll about a year later, around the age of 15, when I found myself looking in the mirror and seeing a still pudgy boy with bad acne and frizzy hair. The acne I could do nothing about; the hair, I guessed, from looking at my father's scalp would cease to be an issue around the age of 25, but the pudginess . . . maybe, finally, I could do something about that. And so the next morning, I got up early with my dad, and strapped on my Keds, and went running with him, a whole half mile. And it hurt, and my lungs burned, and my feet ached, but then I did something that perhaps I remain proudest of, ever, of anything in my whole life: I got up the next morning and did it again.

And thus began my first personal running boom. I ran my way through high school, winning a letter on our cross-country team, doing community races, getting waves from my parents' friends as they drove past me on the roads. I lost weight, a lot of it—in fact, too much. I experienced, for the first time, the addiction of training: running became my Nutella, replacing the real stuff that I wouldn't eat anymore. I still had no athletic skills: couldn't hit or throw a ball; couldn't drain a basket; and Lord knows (He's the only one who does, as I've never tried it again), I couldn't wrestle. But I could run. If Bruce Bennett ever came after me again, he'd have to catch me first.

Like Jef, I've had starts and stops in my athletic career. I slacked off running in college and the years thereafter, picked it up again in my late 20s, and then, under the pressure of marriage and kids and a job, became a casual jogger and then even less than that, my weight creeping up toward 200 pounds, transforming myself again into the pudgy kid whose bulk made such an amusing splat when it hit that vinyl mat so many years before. But my latest, and hopefully last and lasting, running phase came when I approached 40 and realized (1) I was someday going to die, and (2) if I ran a marathon, I wouldn't. I know, but that's how your brain works when you're facing death.

I finished the 2005 Chicago Marathon in just over 4 hours and discovered that instead of being in the very large portion of first-time marathoners who say to themselves, "There, done that, check that off; now it's time to hike in Nepal," I was part of the much smaller cohort who say, "I wonder if I could do that faster." And so it began: I found running partners, experimented with training programs and nutrition, made a schedule, stuck to it, and passed into the land of the Serious Runner. At the '06 Chicago Marathon, I qualified for Boston. In '07, I ran the Boston Marathon.

And now, three and a half years and three more marathons and countless shorter races after that, I am a remarkable thing, something I never expected I would or could be: an athlete.

And in two weeks, I will be something else, if I survive it: a triathlete.

I am writing this foreword less than two weeks before the 2009 Chicago Triathlon, the largest in the world, which will be my first ever. Olympic distance, of course, because if you're going to be stupid, don't go halfway. I will be riding a bike I haven't purchased yet. I will be wearing Jef Mallett's tri wetsuit,[9] which he mailed to me because he is kind and generous and, like all evangelists, lives to make converts.

I am a mediocre cyclist, having never raced at any distance. I am a worse swimmer, having caused many onlookers at the pool to shake their heads in pity. My race plan, such as it is, is to not drown; to not crash; and then, by God, to smoke the bastards on the run, assuming I'm alive. This is poor stuff. But I am doing it, I think, for the same reason that I decided to run that first marathon, or decided to quit my job some years ago and try to be a writer, or moved to Chicago to take a job hosting a struggling public radio program: *because I don't really know if I can.* Because, as it turns out, what I'm nostalgic for, and what I'm trying to re-create, is not that horrible moment of being crushed by Bruce Bennett, all those years

---

9   That's how I know we're the same height, but I'm thicker.

ago, but the moment just before, when I didn't know *what* would happen. When something amazing might be revealed.

After you read this, oh Foreword reader of the future, go Google my name, and if you don't pull up an obituary that mentions drowning or heatstroke or death by apoplexy trying to pull on a wetsuit owned by a cartoonist who's thinner than I, then you will know that at least I survived the experience. Beyond that, I can't tell you what happened—or from my perspective, what will happen. That's the whole point of running, or triathlon, or life. To summarize Jef Mallett's funny, heartfelt, serious work of evangelism that follows this paragraph: the point of triathlon, or anything difficult, is to face your own Bruce Bennett across that mat and find out, again and again, what you're made of. And hope it's not Nutella.

—Peter Sagal
Host of National Public Radio's *Wait Wait . . . Don't Tell Me!*

Editor's Note: Peter finished the 2009 Chicago Triathlon in 2:50:35. He did not drown, did not crash, and smoked the bastards on the run.

TRIZOPHRENIA

The Power of Three

So, a lawyer, a doctor, and a triathlete walk into a bar.
Bartender says, "We don't get many triathletes in here."
Triathlete says, "And at these prices you won't get many more."

Wow! Did you notice what I noticed? (1) That genre of joke always starts with three characters. (2) Like most great stories, it was told in three acts. And (3) you rolled your eyes and protested in three pained, identical syllables: *"Ha. Ha. Ha."*

You did that because the joke has—yes!—three major flaws. (1) It's not really that funny; (2) price never stopped a triathlete from buying anything; and (3) that gag is older than the Father, the Son, and the . . . holy smokes! There it is again!

What is it about the number three? Three dimensions. Three primary colors. Third planet from the sun.

Veni, vidi, vici. Citius, altius, fortius. Hut, hut, hike.

Three wishes. Three blind mice. The three bears. (Am I belaboring this idea too much? Or too little? Or juuuust right?)[1]

And of course: Swim. Bike. Run.

---

[1] One place where the magic of three falls apart is the human body. One heart, one brain, one nose. Two lungs, two eyes, two arms. Then straight to five: five fingers, five toes. Barring some sort of grisly accident, we don't come equipped with three of anything.

Do we?

I was riding bicycles in Tuscany with the kind of friends who know people. Thus, riding with us was one Paolo Guerciotti, a former pro. Paolo wasn't buying into the "former" aspect of anything, at least not on the flats where he and I were riding and conversing. He was young, after all.

"Nineteen!" Paolo said, holding a straight line amid enthusiastic gesturing. "I am nineteen years old!"

Paolo won the Italian national championship in 1978. This was 2004. I may be a writer and an illustrator, but I can do at least that much math. My eyebrows betrayed a little skepticism.

"I am nineteen *each leg!*" he elaborated.

More mental math. More eyebrow action.

More gesturing. "I have-a three legs."

Triathlon.

The sport sounds crazy to outsiders, but you can't argue the numbers. Triathlon has three legs. A tripod has three legs. And what's the signature virtue of a tripod?

Stability.

Yes, stability. People who get off a perfectly good bike to flirt with shin splints are stable. People who leave perfectly good asphalt to play mosh-pit bumper cars in water over their heads are stable. People who leave a liquid, gravity-free environment to spend time with the majority of their weight on the frontmost inch and a half of a bicycle saddle are stable.[2]

There's an enviable balance to a body with a runner's legs, a swimmer's torso, and a cyclist's cuts. And a Zen-like calm to realizing that somehow your order got called in wrong and you ended up with the swimmer's legs and the runner's deltoids, and being fine with that because you get the same heart and lungs and red blood cells either way. Isn't that stability? And if the basis of a sound mind is a sound body, then that mind cannot help but thrive in a body that gets substantially more exercise with a fraction of the single-sport athlete's injury interruptions.

Let us not shortchange that sound mind. While your body adapts to the physical stresses of training, your brain picks up a few tricks as well.

---

2   As with the anatomical footnote, the magic of three is not absolute here. Common practices such as simultaneously talking on a cell phone, grooming, and idling at a traffic light as it goes from red to green and back to yellow are not associated with stability.

It's often argued that that's where the real benefits accrue. Triathlon is not darts. It hurts, and it's time-consuming. To do it right, you have to come up with some toughness. You learn that, as was so eloquently said by former Detroit Tigers manager and English-language mangler Sparky Anderson, "Pain don't hurt." You have to learn focus, and there's nothing like a race and a potential butt-kicking on the horizon to prompt a convergence of priorities. And what of the time needed for all that training, on a planet that stubbornly rotates on a miserly 24-hour schedule? Somehow you find it. If work expands to fit the time allotted, then it seems just as true that wasted time shrinks to fit whatever is left. A track coach once told me that his sprinters got very good at video games and that a lot of his distance runners went on to medical school.

Well, then. Aren't we triathletes awfully impressive people? If so, we're impressive people with an image problem. We wander into the break room at work and mention—with dread, with glee, or as an offhand statement of fact—our upcoming workout, and people don't even finish chewing their potato chips before they say it:

"You're sick."

"You're nuts."

Oh, we're sick, are we? Well, maybe we are. A body that sweats profusely and aches to the bone often *is* sick. Unless it's in perfect health, tapered to peak form, and running at redline. We're insane? Apparently we are. Who but a crazy person would get out of bed well before dawn on a weekend to swallow hard against the butterflies while staring past the start line, over water and mist, to an impossibly distant turnaround buoy?

The truth is, we triathletes wonder ourselves sometimes.[3] I raced my first triathlon not long after the very first Ironman®. Then I quit. Then I started. Then I quit. Then I started again, and now here I am writing about stability.[4]

Maybe it's important to understand that stability is not immovability. Maybe stability is to inertia[5] what courage is to fearlessness—more a triumph over adversity than an absence of it.

Maybe. Always maybe.

Let's explore the maybes. Let's pick triathlon apart and see what we find. Socrates said the unexamined life is not worth living. Maybe the unexamined sport, the unexamined lifestyle—particularly one that's as demanding as this one—is at risk of dissolving into mere routine, and we can't have that. And while we're at it, maybe we can let those heathens in the break room in on the way triathletes think. That worked so well for Socrates.[6]

1. On your mark
2. Get set
3. . . .

---

3   Even something stable is not rock-solid. When renowned architect and control freak Frank Lloyd Wright designed the world headquarters of Johnson Wax in Racine, Wisconsin, he had the chairs built with only three legs. To be fair, instability was kind of the idea, the thought being that it would promote good posture. The effect was that a lot of workers—and by some accounts Wright himself—were dumped on the floor. Today the chairs have four legs, the employees are on their own for posture, and the city of Racine has to look elsewhere for its slapstick.

4   See my cousin Rebecca Gochanour-Stafford-Walton-Caszatt-Charles-Porterhouse's upcoming book about marriage.

5   Inertia is oversold. Whoever said an object at rest remains at rest didn't share a bed with cats, and whoever said an object in motion wants to remain in motion never enjoyed the last 10 kilometers (km) of a marathon.

6   Postapologia tally: 220 jurors voted for acquittal, 280 for the hemlock smoothie.

CHAPTER 1

The Structure of a Sport with a Simple Structure

THE SWIM

L ao-tzu wasn't a triathlete. He was a philosopher some 2,000 or 3,000 years ago. We know he wasn't a triathlete because[1] he's the guy[2] who said that the longest journey begins with a single step. Which a triathlon, our journey of the moment, does not. It begins with a splash, a kick, a rudimentary attempt at a freestyle[3] arm motion, and an intimate encounter with dozens of other oafs' splashes, kicks, and swinging arms. This beginning is followed by a rapid-fire questioning of life, philosophy, and recent decisions that makes Lao-tzu look like a shih tzu.[4]

The triathlon begins with the swim. It nearly always does.

This arrangement is traditional, but it's also pragmatic. Swimming presents an exhausted athlete with the greatest potential for tragedy, so it's good to get it out of the way while everyone's fresh. A broad expanse of water is difficult for lifeguards and officials to patrol, so it's best to

---

1 Lack of triathlons around 500 B.C. notwithstanding.
2 He and 98 out of 100 high school commencement speakers.
3 It doesn't actually have to be freestyle. It can be the crawl, the breaststroke, the sidestroke, or the dog paddle—whatever moves you forward under your own power. Which, come to think of it, is the definition of freestyle. Never mind.
4 A dog known for its coat, its loyalty, and its portability but not for its contributions to deeper thought.

conduct that part of the race before the pack has a chance to stretch out. Food and drink, more of a factor later in the race, are difficult to carry and consume in the water, so there's that. Wetsuits, now common if not ubiquitous, come off a lot faster than they go on.[5]

And let's come right out with it: In the water, no one can tell if you wet your pants.

I'm not saying *you* do that. I'm not saying *I* do. Certainly the guy lined up next to you doesn't. It's bad enough that he's a few minutes away from kicking you in the temple. I'm just saying that, standing on the shore, warmed up, suited up, dripping and shivering, watching the fog rise from the acres of water that will be your home for the next several hundred or thousand breaths of your life, you might feel the urge.

Because that swim is pretty intimidating.

The water is cold, for one thing.[6] And it's big—so very big.[7] That first buoy may be only as far away as a few laps in the pool, but in open water it might as well be the Pitcairn Islands.

The open water[8] is disorienting. There's no dark blue stripe on the bottom of the lake, and even if there were, you'd never see it. Lake water's not quite as clear as the chlorinated stuff in the pool at the YMCA, and even in the most pristine former gravel pit, what sediment does exist will be stirred into a nice, opaque suspension once the thrashing begins.

The thrashing. There's no way around it:[9] The start of the swim at the start of a triathlon is like the front row at an Almighty Lumberjacks of Death[10] concert, only wetter, colder, and, given current trends in wetsuit

---

5   The clock doesn't stop between events. Not while you peel off your wetsuit, change your clothes, stretch, drink, or even while you move from the water to the transition zone, the corral where all your equipment is stored. There are no time-outs, no halftimes, no breaks between innings, no huddles, and no coffee breaks in triathlon.

6   In spite of all that peeing going on.

7   There is no single, official, set distance for a triathlon, but there are some standard benchmarks. An Olympic, or intermediate-distance, race features a 1,500-meter (m) swim. A long-course, or half-Ironman, race has you swim 1.2 miles. An Ironman-distance triathlon, distinct from but the same distance as an Ironman-Registered-Trademark-and-Don't-You-Forget-It triathlon, is of course twice that. A sprint is anything shorter than an Olympic-distance triathlon, usually 400 yards to a half mile. They're all triathlons. All people who have finished one are triathletes.

8   Once in a while they'll have you race in a pool, but it's rare and logistically problematic with a field of any size.

9   Figuratively, anyway. Literally, you can cut down on it by giving the thrashers a 30-second head start or by plotting a course a little on the outer perimeter and away from the mosh pit.

10   Real band. Detroit. Heyday in the late 1980s. Occasional reunions.

graphics, with a marginally smaller portion of the crowd dressed completely in black.

The action stirs the emotions much as it stirs the silt. The starter's horn sounds, and it's not so much a signal as a switch. The glassy water explodes into a boil. Silence to a roar. Your parasympathetic nervous system hands the controls to your sympathetic nervous system, which selects the fight-or-flight knob and shoves it to the firewall. The mild fellow at your side goes from a four-limbed swimmer like you to a six-legged water bug to an eight-tentacled Humboldt squid to a trireme trimmed to ram, and he's getting the same impression of you. Veer to avoid an elbow at starboard and take the heel of a hand from port. Hesitate for the feet probing for a clear shot at the bridge of your nose and you're all but boarded from astern. It stays this way until the first turn. Then everybody tries to cut the corner, and it's twice as bad.

The swim is awful. So awful that it would ruin triathlon if it weren't so wonderful.

Indeed, if it didn't make triathlon what it is.

Part of triathlon's appeal, even as it grows less rare, is that it's still a bit exotic. Runners can picture themselves bicycling. Cyclists can picture themselves running.[11] But swimming is a different matter entirely, and open-water swimming is another step yet. I've talked to more than one[12] elite pool swimmer who says the wide-open stuff makes him feel like a fish out of . . . out of a nice, safe, clean aquarium with lane lines, I suppose.

The swim, then, is the exclusive icing on the exotic cupcake. Put another, less insulin-dependent way, the swim is what gets you out of racing against all those fast runners and cyclists who are too scared to swim or too lazy[13] to learn.

---

11   Looking a lot like a *Tyrannosaurus rex* with chafing issues.

12   From what I've seen of the polling business, this is what's called a "statistically valid sample."

13   Is that the right word? Hard as swimming is, it's not nearly as dependent as other sports on pure fitness. Humans are laughably inefficient in the water. Even the best swimmers of our species are no better than 10 percent mechanically efficient. Most of us can only fantasize that one day 3 percent of our effort will propel us forward while 97 percent manufactures splashes. Technique trumps fitness every time. For the kind of effective example that only humiliation can fully provide, try this: Work yourself into fighting trim and enter a masters swim meet. Lie about your times enough to get seeded into a heat against some former college swimmers who look anywhere from somewhat to substantially older and less chiseled than your pretentious self. Race a few events, and see what happens. Don't worry. They'll wait for you afterward. "But that doesn't fit the image," you may say. "Olympic swimmers look ripped." And indeed they do. Their perfect technique is the product of repetition, and to raise a swim stroke to that level of beauty and efficiency requires a staggering amount of repetition, thou-

Here's where it gets weird: Now that the swim has defined triathlon, its importance within any given triathlon fades. It's typically the shortest part of the race.[14] Since it's the first event of the three, it gives you plenty of opportunities to make up for lost time if you're concerned with that sort of thing. And a certain share of the people ahead of you are there because they're better swimmers than they are cyclists and runners, leaving you with the prospect of a dandy ego boost as you pass them later.

It's an accepted axiom in the sport that you won't win a triathlon in the swim. The painful corollary, though, is that you can sure as hell lose one there, and people do. Irrational exuberance in the water will cost far more in resources than it will return in minutes. If that bill comes due while there's much race left, it's a bad investment of Gatsbyesque proportions.

Digest that a moment. Consider what it means. Until you get fit, and I mean astonishingly fit, with energy to spare at the finish line after miles, perhaps hours, of racing flat out, there's no point in busting your hump on the swim. To do so is, in fact, ill-advised. Moreover, the longer the race, the more that's so. As triathletes go, I am a mediocre swimmer. I clawed my way to that level from pathetic (where, as swim specialists go, I remain).[15] For years, I figured the swim was just the price of admission to a flattering bike ride. And then at some point,[16] the swim became fun. I crossed a threshold where I still wasn't fast, but I was comfortable in the water. I didn't die when I was a much worse swimmer, so it stands to reason I'm not likely to die now. I still wait for the starting horn with a fluttering stomach, but they're butterflies of anticipation rather than moths of dread.[17]

---

sands upon thousands of yards up and down the pool, day in and day out, years on end. Yes, they're fit. But it's almost as if the fitness is the inevitable, happy by-product of all that drilling for technique. So "lazy" may not be the right word, but it's the one I'm sticking with.

14   The person who finished exactly halfway down the standings in the 2008 USA Triathlon national age-group championships for the intermediate distance—is this all sounding median enough?—spent 19.3 percent of her race swimming, as opposed to 49 percent of her time on the bike and 29.3 percent of it running.

15   That reference in note 13 to masters meets? Written less than two weeks after placing fourth from last (50 free), third from last (100 free), fifth from last (200 free), and dead last, behind, among others, a woman my mother's age who had already raced more events that day than I had (500 free).

16   Actually, there's nothing vague about this point. It was during a swim across the Straits of Mackinac, the four-mile-wide channel between Michigan's Upper and Lower Peninsulas. It's safe to say I would not have had the opportunity, the skill, or even a subatomic-level thought of what turned out to be one of the most beautiful experiences of my life if it weren't for triathlon. This is a sport that opens doors.

17   An even better name for a band than the Almighty Lumberjacks of Death, if you ask me.

I'm not facing a trial. I'm looking forward to a pleasant skim over—it's hard to make that much water look ugly—a beautiful tableau. It's a warm-up. No, it's better than that. It's a guilt-free joyride.

On race day it is, anyway. If I've trained and practiced and ground my way through sufficient laps and drills and intervals that were anything but a joyride. And if I make it through another race without taking an elbow to the eye.

Sure, at the elite level, every second will matter. Even at that, the swim may be where those seconds matter least. But you have to have the swim. A competition involving cycling, running, and, say, javelin throwing would still be a disparate triad, maybe even a triathlon. But a triathlon in name only. No swim, no real triathlon.

And there you have it. The swim is terrible. It's beautiful. It's demanding. It's gracious. It is perhaps the least important part of a win but just as arguably the most important part of the race. Like the more deist interpretations of God and a lot of business executives' interpretations of themselves, the swim doesn't have to actually do anything to matter.

It just has to exist.[18]

---

18   Certain executives may not even need to do that.

THE BIKE

Do you remember when you were a kid? That giddy feeling of freedom the day you wove down the road on a two-wheeler for the very first time? The sense of pride and accomplishment? The rush of speed? The certainty that you looked as cool as you'd ever looked in your whole, entire life?

That's how it feels when you begin the bike leg of a triathlon. Except for the giddiness, the freedom, the pride, the accomplishment, the rush, and the coolness.[1] Mostly, you weave.

The swim requires one form of equilibrium management, and the bike requires another, and the time you spend in the transition zone[2] never seems sufficient to fully adjust. Experienced racers get used to it,

---

1   Especially the coolness. I blame aero helmets. Including mine.
2   Anywhere from seconds to a couple of minutes to Just a Minute Honey I'll Be Right Down, depending on preparation, experience, and motivation.

and you probably won't weave as much or as long as you think,[3] but the contrast can be startling.

Contrast indeed. As John Paul Jones[4] never said, "I have not yet begun to point out contrasts."

It begins with a contrast of contrasts itself. The scene before the swim is a chaos of conformity. Racers mill about on the shoreline inside the staging area in a mosaic of different sizes, different shapes, different ages, different genders, different training programs, different motives, different backgrounds, different incomes, and different stories—and they all look the same.[5] Rubber swim cap. Goggles. And formfitting skin, be it neoprene, Lycra, or flesh, black or white or assertively synthetic. Spectators outside the snow-fence pen wave and shout encouragement to no one in particular, unable to pick out blood relatives or the most intimate of friends.

In the transition zone, the bicycles stand in orderly rows of inconsistency. No two bikes look the same. This year's It bike is racked next to a hand-me-down mountain bike, like the boss's Ferrari and the Employee of the Month's Cavalier. They hang by the saddle or handlebars from glorified sawhorses. There's a brand-new road bike on one side; a vintage wire donkey[6] on the other; and somebody's shoes, socks, and water bottles happily emigrating down the row in both directions. The racks repeat themselves, but the bikes keep doing their own thing.

The Smithsonian couldn't assemble a better bicycle museum, and a curator wouldn't know how to catalog the exhibits if it did. Species doesn't follow genus doesn't follow family, and there's no order. It's as if the Westminster Kennel Club co-booked Madison Square Garden with "Show Us Your Mutts."[7]

---

3   Except for those guys who weave and wobble throughout the entire race, most noticeably when you're trying to pass them. That weaving is unrelated to the swim, vertigo, or the personal insult it so closely resembles at the time. Just so you're prepared for it, some people will weave that much and that long, and it won't be because of vertigo. They're just . . . squirrels.

4   I don't mean John Paul Jones, bassist/keyboardist for (the far less creatively named than certain Detroit punk bands) Led Zeppelin. I mean John Paul Jones, commander of the USS *Bonhomme Richard*, who never said that. Had either John Paul Jones said it, he would have said it with a charming accent.

5   Overheard on shore:
     Novice triathlete, fitting his goggles over his eyes, worrying his swim cap into place, and squirming the tighter joints of his wetsuit into submission, to his more experienced friend: "How do I look?"
     Experienced friend: "Like the rest of us."
     Novice triathlete: "Shit."

6   Classic old slang for a bicycle, or slang for an old classic bicycle.

7   I don't know if there is such a show, but I'd sure go.

There are purebreds in the transition zone: bikes that flaunt generations of, if not meticulous breeding, then research and development. They're beautiful. They're well cared for. They're seriously functional and seriously—you could almost say overly—specialized. They are light.[8] They are aerodynamic.[9] They go fast.[10] They are a joy to ride.[11] They are worth the money.[12]

But (to carry this dog-show metaphor perhaps a step further than I should) sometimes Princess gets out of the yard. All too commonly, sleek machines with slippery tubing and carbon-fiber disc wheels sport sloppy, flapping race numbers, a fortune in aerodynamics squandered for want of a few cents' worth of electrical tape. Or check out the barely used rocket ship the 5-foot-3 bargain hunter bought from the 6-foot-2 pro, the saddle peering over the lip of the seat-post collar like the Kilroy Was Here guy.

Down the row, people have been more careful with their crossbreeding. A modest aluminum frame is shod with high-end wheels, a very good move. The bike is a Labrador with a greyhound's legs. Nearby, a moderately priced road bike is hung with a power meter that cost the same amount: a Doberman's heart in a terrier's skin. Look, there's something assembled piece by piece from whatever was on sale: a Welsh corgi.[13]

How to categorize the bikes? Well, you don't. You just ride the hell out of them. You get out of the water, put on your helmet and shoes, roll your bike out of the transition zone, and pedal through whatever vertigo remains from the swim-to-bike contrast.

And you ride on to the next contrast. Cycling is so different from swimming. You go faster. You don't bump into people.[14] You don't even ride that close to other people.[15] It's colder.[16] You have to pay attention to eating and drinking.

And now you have to start thinking seriously about strategy.

---

8   If you are.

9   If you sit on them right.

10   If you've got the suds.

11   If you've got the experience to handle a bike that places your hips forward, your back horizontal, your hands away from the brakes, and a disconcerting amount of your weight over the front wheel.

12   If.

13   I know they're purebreds, but I'm not convinced.

14   Please.

15   The International Triathlon Union (ITU) allows drafting in its races, but unless you're a pro or trying out for the Olympic Games, triathlons don't allow drafting. You're not allowed near another rider unless you're passing or being passed, and you only get a few seconds to make that happen. But get this: Drafting is perfectly legal for swimmers, and it works almost as well. (NB: Drafting, the technique of saving energy by riding closely behind another rider while he or she pushes the majority of the air out of the way, is what makes bicycle racing exciting—and what makes ITU triathlon boring. Just my opinion, and wise people

In the lake, strategy is simple. You get into the water. You get out of the water. Ideally, those two parts take place as close together as possible, but really, that pace has been decided in the pool over the past weeks, months, and years. You get in, you get out. You move on.

On the bike, strategy issues get more complicated. The good news: The bike is the longest part of the race.[17] It offers the most opportunity to gain on the competition. The bad news: It offers the greatest opportunity to overdo it.[18] Meaning, up to a certain point, it's good to ride fast. Beyond that point . . . well, you don't go beyond that point. You stay on the edge, but you don't go faster. Or else you go a good deal faster. Very much faster. Because you're going to want a nice fat cushion when you implode on the run.

And where is that point? As if I know. I only find it occasionally, and I still haven't found it in a half-Ironman.[19] It's a moving target. It depends on your preparation, the weather, the terrain, how you feel that day. Certainly on your overall strengths and weaknesses, and even on whether you're riding the hot bike or the hoopty. It has a lot to do with the distance of the race.[20] In a short enough sprint or even an Olympic-distance triathlon, you may be able to redline it the whole way and have enough left for the correspondingly short run. Maybe. Maybe not. *Do you feel lucky? Do you, punk?*[21]

You are lucky. You're riding the bike leg of a triathlon, and it doesn't get much better than that. You're between the part that's scary and the part that's painful. You're going fast. You're playing with one of your favorite toys, and you're justifying all the money[22] you spent on it.

---

disagree. ITU-style, draft-legal racing essentially keeps the competitors together until the run, which can be handy for the casual spectator and damned convenient for the film crews [see "Olympic Games," prev.]. But I'm not writing about casually watching triathlons or filming them. I'm writing about racing in them, and a triathlon with drafting is essentially a footrace with two predictable warm-up acts.)

16   Yes, it is. Cold as it was to jump into that water, consider the prospect of a 20-odd mph wind while soaked from head to toe in that same water. Maybe the air will be warm enough not to chill you, but given the time of day they tend to start these things, don't count on it.

17   In the case of our friend in the age-group nationals, 49 percent of the race.

18   Not to mention the greatest temptation. A relatively strong cyclist/weak swimmer passing a line of strong swimmers/weak cyclists is the most judgment-impairing combination this side of spring break and tequila.

19   Four for five in meltdowns at that distance. Also four for five in zippy bike splits and a "See me" note from the professor in Pattern Recognition 101.

20   Olympic- or intermediate-distance race: 40 km, just shy of 25 miles. Sprint: anything less than that. Ironman: 112 miles; half-Ironman: 56 miles.

21   Clint Eastwood as Dirty Harry, of course. The line is as familiar as Lao-tzu's, and nearly as old.

22   Most of the money. Nobody's perfect.

You're turning the pedals in a steady cadence, you're focusing on the horizon, and your brain is gradually jettisoning any thoughts that don't pertain to the task at hand. A person so inclined might even say you're meditating.

You're forgetting to drink.

Now you're remembering to drink, and your tepid electrolyte-and-sugar solution tastes like champagne.[23]

You're gliding down a country road that is light on cars, effectively free of stop signs, and lined with appealing scenery and supportive fans.[24]

You are alive.

And you look great.

Actually, you're dressed funny, and you're drooling. But anyone close enough to tell you so is close enough to get busted for drafting.

---

23 No, it doesn't. I got carried away.
24 And baffled locals.

THE RUN

We had to learn to swim. We had to learn to ride a bike. But[1] we were born to run.

You've survived the swim. You've racked your bike, left your hardware behind,[2] and hit the homestretch unencumbered in the most natural mode of locomotion possible. It only sounds simple. Somewhere between the bike and the run, everything changes. The bike leg of a triathlon is Spartan in its intensity and Spartan in its efficiency—and then, right before the run, it's not. In the last mile, your linear focus frays like an old brake cable. Now you're multitasking. You're shifting down a gear and spinning your legs loose while you try to ignore the rider ahead whom you've been determined to pass. You're taking a last good drag

---

1   Baby, . . .

2   Eventually. Sometimes it takes a few tries. If—no, *when*—you volunteer at a triathlon instead of racing in it, one of the best postings is at the exit of the transition zone heading onto the run course. You'll enjoy reminding a surprising number of athletes that they no longer need to wear their helmets. You'll enjoy it out of empathy more than anything because if you haven't done it yourself, you can remember how close you've come.

from your water bottle and one final hit of gel. Maybe you're undoing the Velcro straps and pulling your feet out of and on top of your shoes. You're trying to remember where your slot is in a transition area that suddenly looks like the Mall of America parking lot the weekend before Christmas. You're visualizing how you've laid out your gear over your 18 inches of real estate and wondering how it can be so complicated to remember two shoes, two socks, a number belt, and a hat. Out of nowhere, the solution to the Middle East problem occurs to you, and you file it away for later because right now you're negotiating a maze of orange cones and signs on sticks and a maelstrom of volunteers waving to you to go this way to more cones and that way to more volunteers and finally to the stripe on the pavement and the very big orange cones and the most frantic volunteers of all, waving and yelling to stop, stop right here, dismount before this line and walk your bike, and for God's sake you can't be expected to remember where your stuff is and how you laid it out at the same time, not that it matters because it's been kicked around by a couple of other racers who overcooked it on the bike and are even more addled than you. People are still fighting like toddlers with Stinger missiles in the cradle of civilization, so no one's going to blame you if you try to run with your helmet on.

Right about now, the only thing more unnatural than the runner sporting a helmet is the simple mechanics of running. It feels like you're operating your legs by remote control. No, not even that. It feels like you're using someone else's legs. Someone who, it turns out, isn't much of a runner.

It's not just you. Everybody's running on somebody else's legs. Usually Groucho Marx's. Never a Kenyan's, for some reason. All you know is that whoever got yours, you'd like to have them back.

You do get your own legs back. But how soon?[3]

How soon depends on your preparation, your bike effort, and even your bike itself. First, your preparation. We humans evolved legs for running and brains for designing bicycles, and from there we evolved legs that could pedal as well, but we never quite evolved legs that could do one after the other in quick succession.[4] That's something we have to condition ourselves to do. It's a simple process: You just practice. You ride a bike, and then you get off and run, and the more you do that, the

---

3   And who had them? Was it the Leg Valet, returning them to you warmed up and babied and even polished here and there? Or was it the Leg Teenaged Son, returning them to you popping and hissing and with very little gas in the tank?

4   Darwin didn't spend a lot of time on this issue, which is fine because the last thing we need is for this book to be banned in Dogma County, Kansas.

easier it gets come race day. Triathletes even have a word for this specific drill: brick. Kind of a funny name, isn't it? Supposedly[5] it's one of those forced acronyms that become a whole new word, like SCUBA[6] or SNAFU[7] but more forced: *bike and run in combination.*[8] Forced, maybe, but very descriptive of the feeling the transition imbues in your legs.[9] Any coach or book or blog will be happy to outline a specific brick regimen, but really a brick is to training what the swim leg is to a triathlon: How you do it is not nearly as important as *that* you do it.

What you did on the bike affects the first part of your run, too. It doesn't take an advanced degree from MIT to figure out[10] that the more you wear yourself out on the bike, the less energy you'll have to run with. And the harder you mash down on the pedals, the more your muscles stay in that mode when you'd rather they loosen up and allow you to run like a normal person. A triathlon-specific bike can minimize this problem a bit. Aside from the funny handlebars and the teardrop tubing and the deep-section rims and the frontal surface area of a fashion runway model, the real value is that the seat tube—the one that goes from the pedals to the saddle—is positioned at a much more vertical angle than that on a standard road bike. This alteration offers more aerodynamic gains, allowing you to bend over further without slugging your chest with your knees, but its real value is that it recruits slightly different muscles, sending you out on the run course with muscles that are a little more warmed up and a little less worn-out.

But ultimately, it's the bricks. The more you practice bricks, the easier the first part of the run will be. And the more you hammer the bike course, the more bricks you'll wish you'd done.

That awkward transition sounds like nothing but trouble, but I'll give it this: It keeps you from going out too fast.[11] You've still got some racing to do. And you're about done being comfortable anyway, so enjoy the variety.

---

5   Noah Webster not having devoted a whole lot more ink to multisport than Darwin.

6   Self-contained underwater breathing apparatus.

7   Look it up yourself. I'm already getting threatening mail from the Dogma County Courthouse.

8   The K is not only silent but reclusive.

9   Or arms. A brick has come to define any two or even all three disciplines in succession, but the bike-run sequence is the most vital and also makes the best acronym, forced as it is. *Swim and bike in combination* just comes out looking like a typo or a phone company, and *swim now and footrace ultimately* was already taken by the military.

10   Nothing in this book does; an astonishing relief to the author.

11   In 1511, King Henry VIII's favorite battleship, the *Mary Rose*, left port to kick some French arse and promptly tipped over and sank as England watched from shore.

Let me pause here to bust a myth or two about distance. Specifically, the idea that one distance is harder or more impressive than another. How hard they are is up to you, not the guy who designs the course. An Ironman, with its 2.4-mile swim, 112-mile bike, and 26.2-mile run, most certainly is hard. That's a long trip, and it's going to take some training. I wouldn't recommend it for anyone's first triathlon. But an Olympic-distance race, at 1,500 m, 40 km, and 10 km, is by no means any less a triathlon or less an accomplishment. The same goes for a sprint. Truth be told, when I did my first Ironman, what struck me wasn't how hard it was but how easy. Until it got very, *very* hard. That local sprint race won't last as long as the high-profile Ironman—maybe not even as long as the painful part—but it will burn the whole way.[12]

The idea is to finish any race the way Pheidippides ran into Athens from Marathon: on the last wisp of fumes.[13] And if the race is so short and you're so fit that you can't drain the tank, then you spend the whole race just a few revolutions per minute shy of throwing a rod. Our bodies have gauges and alarms to tell us when we're approaching these danger zones, just as our cars do. But where our cars have dials and lights, we have personal instrument panels that are calibrated in pain and discomfort.[14]

Triathletes run toward those warnings, not away from them. Does that make sense? Why would anyone deliberately court pain? We're familiar with these questions. We've heard them before, all too often from people who, not to be too blunt, could look down and answer their own question. But you can maintain a certain level of fitness without distress.

Maybe the pain has something to offer us. Herman Melville wrote in *Moby Dick* that a man cannot be truly comfortable unless he has some discomfort to compare his comfort to. He had a point.[15] There's a certain luxury in being able to say you've survived worse.

But I think ultimately, we run simply because we can. Running was our first stab at freedom,[16] and we're moved to celebrate it as long as we can. It's poignant that the run is the last stretch of the triathlon because all too often it's the first thing to go. A friend, an elite mountain bike

---

That kept the *Mary Rose* from overdoing it before engaging the enemy. Maybe this isn't such a good allegory.

12   Like a blowtorch. Compare this to the hot coals at the end of a long-course race and choose your poison. That's what I'm talking about.

13   Sure, he died—there's that. But he'd have died of something by now, anyway.

14   Which hardly seems fair. But then, given that we're inclined to ignore warnings that hurt, we might not be the best candidates for more subtle cues.

15   Which he expressed in one of history's most exciting books, of which about 75 percent is filler and digression with no action to speak of. Melville knew about contrast.

16   Ask your parents.

racer, says cycling is the catch basin for expired runners. And swimming has broken the fall of many an injured cyclist. So we run because we can. And maybe we run so long because someday we can't.

And if it hurts, is that wrong? John Steinbeck had the right idea: "I have always taken my hangovers as a consequence, not as a punishment." What a hangover pain is. What a bender running is.

We know the warning gauges are set conservatively, that we're not going to pull a Pheidippides. And that long zone between first warning and breakdown comprises a world of self-discovery. They say character is forged in a furnace of pressure, pain, and peril,[17] but for my money, pain suffices. Especially triathlon pain because it's totally under your control. You quit, the pain quits. You have a choice. But it's a choice, not a question. You know the answer, and knowing it isn't enough. You have to enact it.

"Choice" sounds awfully instantaneous for an event that can last hours, and I still haven't reconciled the confusion. My coach always said the way through the pain was to stay in the moment. Really? But that's where the pain is. George Carlin said no such moment exists anyway. "There's no present," he said. "There's only the immediate future and the recent past."

I'd never have bet on George Carlin to beat my coach in a race, but I like his timetable. I like having a future to run toward. That's where the finish line is. That's where the next race starts. That's where your friends and family hug your salty, sweaty self and strangers cheer. Where there's fresh fruit and yogurt near the results and a dry shirt in your goody bag. It's where you belong.

It's the only place you were ever headed.

---

17 And peas. Eat your peas.

CHAPTER 2

A Brief History of a Sport with a Brief History

WHEN IT STARTED

aseball Hall of Fame pitcher Satchel Paige famously said, "Don't look back. Something might be gaining on you."

I don't know much about baseball,[1] but I know enough about triathlon to say that we're the kings of not looking back. Partly because, triathlon bikes being set up the way they are and handling the way they do, looking back is only going to make you steer straight into whatever is gaining on you. But in the broader sense, we don't look back much because there's just not that much to see.

Triathlon is, as far as the more serious sports go, young. By young, I mean babbling, drooling, unsteadily walking, unable-to-eat-solid-foods young. And that's not really a metaphor. That's a bang-on-the-money description of me at the end of the 2007 Toyota Challenge half-Ironman in Deer Creek, Ohio. And triathlon is younger than I am.

---

1   Starting with how anyone is going to gain on a pitcher from behind. There is no baseline between second base and the pitcher's mound.

Exactly how young is open to interpretation.[2] Did it start with the first Ironman, in Hawaii? That was in 1978. But that Ironman was founded by one John Collins, who had raced in the San Diego Track Club's First Annual Mission Bay Triathlon. That race was in 1974, and it was the first to call itself a triathlon. But it, in turn, was founded in part by

---

2   Just like Satchel Paige! His birth year is estimated, but only estimated, to be 1905, give or take. He said a lot of great things, including "How old would you be if you didn't know how old you are?" If Satchel Paige were alive, he would be a lot older than the sport of triathlon.

Jack Johnstone, who essentially just added a bike leg to the Dave Pain[3] Birthday Biathlon, a run-swim event that debuted in 1972.

The Dave Pain biathlon was distantly preceded by a whole different type of biathlon, of course, the one that retains the name. That biathlon combines Nordic skiing and shooting rifles. It debuted as an organized sport in 1776 in Norway but hearkens back to big, hairy Scandinavians either hunting or fighting,[4] both of which started when somebody was too busy to make a note of the time.[5]

And we've all heard of the decathlon, that 10-event pastiche that is the heart and soul of the Olympic Games, which made its first Olympic appearance in 1912[6] in Stockholm.[7] To be fair, the ancient Olympians had their own multisport event, but for them, counting on just one hand was enough,[8] and they kept it at the pentathlon level. That pentathlon is not to be confused with the modern pentathlon,[9] which debuted at the same Stockholm Olympics and now bears little resemblance to triathlon other than to make the latter appear both logical and inexpensive.[10]

So, yeah. The Olympics. Triathlon is an Olympic sport. You probably knew that. You may not have known that it went from zero to Olympic faster than any other sport. If you take the accepted view that the Mission Bay triathlon in San Diego was the first, that means it was only 26 years before the sport made it into the 2000 Sydney Olympics. I know people with handlebar tape older than that.[11]

---

3   His real name! How cool is that?

4   Like so many sports.

5   Kind of tips the odds toward fighting, if you ask me.

6   So, heart and soul, maybe, but not distant heritage.

7   Vikings again! Less big and hairy at that point.

8   The other hand having been broken in a wrestling match.

9   Dig it: (1) shooting, (2) fencing, (3) swimming, (4) horseback riding (on a borrowed horse provided by the promoter and assigned by lottery, no less), and (5) cross-country running. The idea is to simulate the situation of a military officer caught behind enemy lines, first fighting, then fleeing across the river, then stealing a horse, and finally running home after the horse gets shot out from underneath him. It's not a precursor to triathlon so much as it's a precursor to Grand Theft Auto.

10 Although, considering the lack of resemblance, triathlon and modern pentathlon have a surprising amount in common, starting with the military angle. The previously noted John Collins, founder of the original Ironman triathlon, was a U.S. Navy commander. The winner of that first race, Gordon Haller, was a former military pentathlete, and he came around John Dunbar, a former navy SEAL, for the victory. And in Beijing in 2008, former world triathlon champion Sheila Taormina became the first woman to compete in the Olympics in three separate sports: swimming, triathlon, and modern pentathlon.

11 . . . Dad.

Not that the Olympics are quite the pinnacle they used to be.[12] They are, frankly, getting a little crowded and commercial and perhaps less than aggressively selective. These days, being in the Olympics gives your sport credibility like being in the Mall of America gives your pretzel cart credibility. But triathlon is there, and it looks poised to stay there without the kind of controversy and smirking that have shadowed other recent additions and proposed additions. It's just got that whole *citius, altius, fortius*, old-school Olympic feel to it. It feels legitimate. It's even got its own world governing body (the ITU) and national governing bodies (USA Triathlon in the United States) and the boring political squabbles that go with such organizations.

And triathlon is growing. How much it's growing is open to all sorts of claims and support that are subject to manipulation,[13] drift, and somnolence, and there are more tangible clues, anyway. You don't have to live in Southern California or Boulder anymore to find a triathlon. In fact, if you live near any kind of population base, you can find a race within a reasonable drive most weekends during the triathlon season. Even in a country where it is increasingly common to physically resemble a ripe persimmon without ever consuming one, an entry into some of the more prestigious triathlons can be a tougher score than tickets to a Beatles reunion.[14] Perhaps most telling is that most American of barometers: retail sales. You can buy triathlon-specific stuff. Not just bikes but also accessories and clothing—and they're easy to find. Triathletes can race in fast-drying, aerodynamic clothing that can be worn start to finish instead of improvising with a Speedo the size and pattern of a Peter Max commemorative postage stamp.[15] Um.[16]

Triathlon is growing because it deserves to.

And not because it's in the Olympics, and not because another professional won the Ironman world championship in Kona or the ITU world championship or even took home the big prize money from some other race.

It's growing because it's within driving range and training range, and because finishing a triathlon sounds impressive even though just about anybody can do it if they put in the work. It sounds impressive because it *is* impressive even though just about anybody can do it if they put in

---

12   This might just be me on a rant.
13   "Who are you going to believe, me or your lies, damn lies, and statistics?" A rant made famous by Mark (or should I say "Marx") Twain.
14   Though probably less fraudulent.
15   This may be as much a source of triathlon's success as an indicator.
16   Peter Max? Of all the artists in the world for the tiny Speedo joke, I had to choose Peter Max?

the work. It's because the cross-training integral to that work sculpts the body into something a little closer to parts that match and a little less likely to be held together with tape and ibuprofen. It's because you can race on the same course, on the same day, as the national champion or your rookie friend. Or both at the same time.

It's growing not because of the first triathlon in San Diego in 1974, or the first Ironman in 1978, or the first Olympic triathlon in 2000. It's growing because of the next triathlon in your life.

We're triathletes. We look forward much better than we look back.

Although I did look back once, and do you know what I saw? Satchel Paige, that's what.[17] But that was toward the end of the 2007 Toyota Challenge, and I was seeing all sorts of things.

---

17   And he said, "Ain't no man can avoid being born average, but there ain't no man got to be common." So I really couldn't stop, you see.

HOW IT STARTED

While acknowledging that kids have been riding their Schwinns to the ol' swimmin' hole since Norman Rockwell watched them go, we'll give the San Diego Track Club credit for the eureka moment. After all, it's one thing to be first and another to be followed.

The specifics: 6 miles of running, 5 miles of bicycling, and 500 yards of swimming.[1]

The charm: This was California Mellow at its finest. Jack Johnstone and Don Shanahan dreamed up the race after the Dave Pain biathlon in July, announced it in the club's September newsletter, and held it September 25. That was a Wednesday, selected by default because all the weekends had filled up. Meaning an evening event, leaving late finishers to cross the line to the glow and guidance of the earlier finishers' car headlights. The three disciplines were not only weird distances by today's standards, they weren't even divided into the now customary[2] three legs. It

---

1   That's San Diego *Track* Club. You didn't think it would be heavy on the run?

36   2   And, uh, logical.

was as if someone spilled a box of triathlon parts on the floor, scooped up the broken pieces,[3] and made a race out of them. The race announcement reminded competitors to bring their own bicycles. Attendance smashed expectations—46 starters! On a school night! The entry fee was[4] a buck.

Awards were presented to the top five finishers, and so it was that the Dude from the Trophy Shop became the catalyst for that year's contribution to the English language. He called Johnstone: "How do you spell triathlon?" Johnstone realized it wasn't in any dictionary. He'd invented a new word. He spelled it like the words he'd cobbled it from: Decathlon. Heptathlon. Pentathlon. Biathlon. Triathlon. It's in the dictionary now.[5]

It even has a synonym, or so you'd think: Ironman.[6]

Three years after that first Mission Bay triathlon, a dozen or so runners were arguing at the awards banquet following a race around Oahu. They couldn't agree on which sport produced the fittest athletes. You know, the same thing athletes argue about now. But now we have wattage meters and lactate thresholds and VO_2maxes and product endorsements. Back then, they just had common sense, and it was provided by John Collins, who had been one of the 46 charter triathletes in San Diego.[7] Here is what common sense looked like that day: They would merge the three signature one-day endurance events in Hawaii[8] into a single event and let the swimmers take on the cyclists take on the runners. They would combine the Waikiki Roughwater Swim, the Around-Oahu Bike Race,[9] and the Honolulu Marathon, or at least their distances.[10] Collins suggested they call the winner an "iron man." He didn't have to tell anybody how to spell that.[11]

You wouldn't have thought that would be the start of something big. You wouldn't have thought it in large part because you wouldn't have had a clue it was going on. Hawaii isn't exactly on the way to anywhere, and with 15 racers spread out over 140.6 miles, you might not have known

---

3   The longest stretch of running was 2.8 miles. Another section of the run was exactly 2 miles but was run barefoot. The bike was the only leg completed in one unbroken effort, and the race ended with the swim.

4   Johnstone thinks.

5   Added to Webster's dictionary, ninth edition, in 1983.

6   "Ironman" is a synonym for "triathlon" much as "Coca-Cola" is a synonym for "soft drink."

7   He took 35th place out of 46.

8   Kind of ruining it for the Nordic skiing advocates.

9   Forget that earlier qualifier; the Around-Oahu Bike Race was originally a two-day event.

10 Hence the initially random-seeming distances.

11 Although you may be told not to spell anything too close to it in the name of your race or your product; Ironman is a valuable trademark.

you'd seen anything if you *had* stumbled across it. But it was addictive enough for the racers that a year later, 15 competitors[12] lined up again. This time somebody did stumble across it. Sportswriter Barry McDermott was on the island to cover a golf tournament[13] for *Sports Illustrated*, and someone tipped him off to the weirdo endurance freaks. McDermott's 10-page piece in turn tipped off the rest of the world, most notably the offices of ABC's *Wide World of Sports*. They asked if they could cover the race. Collins gave them permission and a caution: "It's about as exciting as watching a lawn-growing contest." ABC was there the next year,

---

12   Including Lyn Lemaire, who would become the first Ironman woman.
13   Which I wonder if anyone remembers at all.

though Collins wasn't,[14] and it turned out it was easier to stumble across a race when it was on national TV.

The race grew, and drama happened. More to the point, drama happened on television. In 1982, a college student named Julie Moss entered the race to gather data for her exercise physiology thesis.[15] She got some. By the time she could see the finish line, she was dangerously fatigued and dehydrated. Her legs gave out, and she crawled—really, literally, crawled—the last few yards to the line while Kathleen McCartney ran past her for the women's title.[16] Moss's struggle was the new triathlon gestalt: You finish, you're a champion.[17] We're still awfully impressed by the guys who come in first, make no mistake. We try to eat what they do, train like they do, buy the same kind of gear they do. But it's the Julie Mosses we relate to.

The Ironman moved from Waikiki to Kona because it had gotten too big for Honolulu traffic, and then it went worldwide because it had gotten too big for just Hawaii. Around the same time, the San Diego Track Club stopped sponsoring triathlons because it stopped having to. The idea had gotten out, and people who wanted to try the sport no longer had to fly to the race in Hawaii or put on their own.

While the idea of the ultimate endurance athlete moved full steam ahead on the Ironman line, promoters elsewhere figured out that the more approachable California model had its merits, too: A triathlon could be worthwhile and worth bragging rights without taking the better part of a day, a year, a marriage, or a savings account. Events popped up all over the place—a Tinman here, an endurathon there, here a fest, there a tri, everywhere triath-a-li.[18]

Distance, order, and format were wide open. The sport was brand-new; anything was fair game. Promoters approached it like stray dogs in a dump, trying one thing, discarding another, and rolling in everything. Maybe the clock kept running between sports; maybe it didn't. Maybe you could draft other cyclists; maybe the promoter didn't know what drafting was. Maybe the three sports were as lopsided as a ten-speed with a sidecar. Maybe they weren't necessarily swimming, cycling, and running, and maybe they didn't add up to three. It was a strange kind of glory

---

14 The navy had transferred him to Washington, DC, presumably not for a job having anything to do with public relations.

15 Today a multimillion-dollar sports industry, in 1982 a homework project.

16 Oy. What are you going to do?

17 Curiously, this ethic didn't catch on in the homework department as well as it did in the triathlon department.

18 Some-a-day soon, I'm op-a-timistic, we can convince the world to drop-a that superfluous -a-.

days, when the sport was too young for its own specialists. Everybody was leaving a comfort zone[19] and trying something new, shopping around for a race that favored their strengths or kicked their asses.[20] In those nascent years, body types varied as much as clothing, which varied like jargon, methods, and feeding habits. You half expected the swim to take you past the HMS *Beagle*, at anchor, Charles Darwin leaning over the gunwale taking notes.

But triathlon is no Galapagos Islands. No boundaries were going to contain its genes. Species inevitably crossed, migrated, specialized, and homogenized to some extent, and the sport followed. When the ITU formed in 1989, one of its first orders of business was to hammer out a standard. The 1.5 km/40 km/10 km recipe was an inspired, balanced ratio, and it remains the most popular distance as measured by the number of triathlons employing it. Triathlon still has its uncategorizable platypus here and there and some crossbreeds that bloom into their own registry.[21] But the sport has stabilized.

Stable doesn't mean stale. Triathlon draws from too broad a population for that. Stability means you can enter a race with the confidence that it will be run by people with access to a history of what works and doesn't work. It means you can expect distances, if not conditions, with which to compare one race to another. You can aspire to national championships if that's your thing, or world championships. You can expect support from sponsors who know what they can expect. You can expect to sign a legal release form that takes longer to read than a treadmill workout on a sunny day[22] and an entry fee somewhat higher than the buck they charged in San Diego in '74. It's an imperfect sport, after all.

And what's wrong with imperfect? One's reach should exceed one's grasp. Robert Browning said something like that. So did my swim coach.

---

19   Pool, road, track, sofa.
20   Frequently, predictably, yet always astonishingly both.
21   The popular and burgeoning half-Ironman distance being the ultimate Labradoodle of the sport.
22   Both of which you will skip.

WHY IT STUCK

his would be a good time to talk about the Shakers.

The Shakers, in their words, were the United Society of Believers in Christ's Second Appearing. They splintered from an English Quaker group in the mid-eighteenth century. Some of them emigrated to America, where the sect did quite well for a while. Their numbers were good, with as many as 6,000 sprinkled throughout the Northeast and Midwest by the 1840s. The Shakers were, by all accounts, a happy people. They were peaceful, social, healthy, and fit. They had firm beliefs but were open to and tolerant of others' beliefs. They were hardworking and, though frugal, hardly deprived. They grew their own food and cooked it wonderfully. They were devoted to their lifestyle. They were self-sustaining.

They were celibate.

Seriously, they did not believe in sex or procreation as a part of life. That's the sort of policy that can have an adverse effect on membership. You're not going to grow the ranks from within, and it's not a real motivator when you're recruiting from outside.

Now would be a good time to swing this discourse back around to triathlon. Like the Shakers, triathletes once numbered 6,000.[1] Like the Shakers, we have been described as a little bit cultish. Like the Shakers, we tend to be a fit, happy, hardworking demographic. Not at all like the Shakers, we now number more than 6,000,[2] and they number less.[3]

It's all well and good for a sport to have its devoted, even addicted core of loyalists, but if you don't make your deal appealing to newcomers, you're going the way of the Shakers.

I have some experience racing triathlons. But more germane to this section, I have all sorts of experience starting out in the sport. I've done it several times.[4] Nobody is more qualified to comment on the appeal of triathlon to beginners.

I shouldn't be so well qualified. I'd like to think of myself as an I'll-try-anything-once guy, not an I'll-quit-the-same-sport-multiple-times guy. I shouldn't even be the I'll-try-anything-once guy. I have a tendency to not get things right the first time.[5, 6]

---

1   Sometime in 1987.

2   A lot more. Like, according to USA Triathlon in 2007, more than 100,000 annual members plus more than 200,000 one-day memberships.

3   A lot less. Like, according to the *Boston Globe* in 2006, exactly four.

4   Before you say it: Don't call me ADD. Attention deficit disorder is a medical term for a medical condition, not a slur for or quick dismissal of a peculiar set of character flaws. Which I have out the wazoo. I believe the proper term for me is "flake."

5   First case study: June 2000, Minneapolis. I've been an editorial cartoonist long enough to attend the Association of American Editorial Cartoonists' annual convention in Minneapolis. I begin the weekend by talking politics with another attendee who looks familiar but whom I cannot place. Rather than just ask who he is, I put my faith in bullshit. I remind him what a fan I am, how I respect his cartoons, and probe for clues with questions about how things are at his newspaper, anyway—and which newspaper is that again? He pauses before answering. "I'm Walter Mondale," says the former vice president and presidential candidate.

6   Second case study: It is 2005, and I'm in rural Nevada closing out the first day of the Nevada Passage, a made-for-TV adventure race. I'm one of 20 competitors who don't know doodly about each other, and I don't know it, but I'm about to introduce myself. I'm chatting it up with the chief timekeeper about rural Nevada cultural curiosities, and the conversation has turned to brothels. My new friend reveals that those businesses are surprisingly welcoming to men who just want to lean in the door and have a look, and if I'm really interested in the local culture, the, ah, bus driver somehow knows the way to the Pussycat Ranch. And would I be interested? Now, there are moments when you've got something to say to just one single person even though you're in a loud crowd, say, a crowd of people you really haven't met but are about to spend a week with. And sometimes that crowd shuts up all at once, say, at the very moment you answer, "There is no way I'm going to northern rural Nevada and *not* visiting a cathouse."

All of which makes me more suited to talk about triathlon's appeal. See if one of the reasons I took up the sport doesn't sound potentially like you.[7]

First start-up: circa 1981
Because triathlon is cool and exotic and individual
I had figured out that I loved sports and even competition, but I didn't much care for either in the context of high school. Mostly I did mildly post-Rocky-Mountain-high, post-post-hippie stuff like backpacking, rock climbing, and riding my bicycle all over Northern Michigan. But then I saw an article in *Sports Illustrated*, by Barry McDermott, about these mildly obsessed endurance athletes in Hawaii. That was it. Triathlon had to be my sport, and this Ironman thing would one day be my race. Once I learned how to swim, anyway. So I got busy. A year later, I heard rumblings of a triathlon being organized a little farther north in Traverse City. There would be a 1-mile swim, a 30-mile bike, and a 10-km run. The bike and run would be extremely hilly, whereas the swim would merely be extremely cold.

I did well. Top ten, in fact, out of a good-sized crowd even by today's standards. I had talent. I was Ironman bound. In reality, I did not and was not. My splits said it all. I don't remember the numbers, but I remember things like being nearly last out of the water, cold enough that my fingers couldn't work the drawstring on my swimsuit, not that changing into bike shorts in my state seemed like the best idea, anyway.[8] My run was an exercise in cramp management and holding on. But that bike split . . .

Maybe bike racing was my sport.

Second start-up: circa 1989
Because triathlon welcomes incompetents, or
Because I'm afraid to go back to bike racing
Bike racing was swell. It was just about as exotic and obscure as triathlon was in that pre-Lance, pre-LeMond era, so I could train without imposing any kind of pressure on my flaky self. I could be pretty good at it if I trained enough. Which I couldn't seem to manage once I started working long hours and got married. The flakiness returned. I pictured people pointing and wondering what on earth had happened to me. And they did, but not at the races. Just in general.

---

7   Be forewarned that "so much natural ability and potential that the only question was whether to become a professional triathlete or join the U.S. Navy SEALs" does not turn up in the mix. On the other hand, if that's you, you're just reading the book to kill time between championships or classified missions anyway.

8   Not being a Shaker and all.

After a few years, work and life stabilized, and I got some fitness back. Should I race bikes again? I should not. While I was forgetting how to race, everybody else was getting better at it.

But triathlon was coming into its own. The Ironman was drawing more than 1,300 racers and dangling a $150,000 prize list in front of them. Smaller races were showing up all over the country. People were using these funny aero handlebars and steering with their elbows. Nobody knew me. No pressure.

Turns out the triathletes my age had been getting better in my absence, just like the bike racers, but nobody thought the worse of me. In fact, though I don't intend to malign cycling,[9] triathletes were a million times friendlier than bike racers.[10] Also, there was always a table full of great food after the race. I was back home. I started to think about the Ironman again. Which, it turns out, is a dangerous thing to do when most of your fitness comes from bicycling and you don't have a lot of patience or smarts. Boy, stress fractures hurt.

Third start-up: circa 1994
Because the hell with the Ironman

After I healed, I moved my attention away from competition altogether. My wife has multiple sclerosis (MS), and she had gone through a bad stretch that left her first unable to run, then unable to balance a bike. I got a little perspective, and the two of us got a tandem.[11] She stayed fit, and I enjoyed her company. We took some great trips. I probably should have left well enough alone. But I noticed I trained more consistently and stayed a lot healthier[12] when I had an event looming. I thought maybe I'd just do a short race here and there. I didn't need to do the full Ironman distance to be a triathlete, and frankly, I really kind of liked going fast. One or two sprint or Olympic races a year wouldn't hurt.

Fourth start-up: circa 2003
Because it fits my life

One or two races a year didn't hurt, but falling down the steps sure did, and the subsequent ankle reconstruction didn't do wonders for my confidence

---

9   Bike racers really aren't any less friendly than triathletes, but it sure looks that way on race day. And I for one understand the game face. A triathlon is an individual sport; a finish can be as good as a win, and an outright win is just a matter of going faster. A bike race is a me-against-you affair. It's a completely different approach to racing. Plus no food table.

10   Than just about anybody! Darn good-looking, too.

11   This is a great purchase. MS not required.

12   Physically and mentally. The connection is not breaking news.

that I'd run well again. I healed, said good-bye to running and triathlon,[13] took the aero extensions off the handlebars, and picked up bike racing again. I was over 35 and could race with the masters, who turned out to be the same guys I'd raced with the first time around but with more experience. Still, I enjoyed it and did pretty well until the mononucleosis.

While I was out with mono, I returned in earnest to another neglected passion: cartoons. Editorial cartoons led to[14] my proposing a comic strip,[15] which turned out to be the second thing[16] I was able to do right on the first attempt. I was able to quit my day job after only a year or two of working 90 hours a week. When life again stabilized, sure enough, sports beckoned. But not bike racing. I was self-employed, and I worked with my hands, and bike racers crash. A broken collarbone or thumb would have been disastrous.[17] And there was still the tandem. If I didn't ride, my wife didn't ride. Bike racers race all the time.[18] Triathletes can[19] pace out their season instead of racing every weekend. Racing triathlons meant never having to say, "Not tonight, honey; I've got a bike race."

Fifth start-up: circa 2007
Really more of a reenlistment

I wouldn't say I found my comfort zone, because I kept improving, and I don't tend to improve when I'm comfortable. It was more that I realized I was confident in my direction. Also, if I was comfortable with a pattern of mediocre finishes wrapped around front-of-the-pack bike splits, then I hadn't learned a damn thing since that first race up in Traverse City. It was time to say good-bye to the bike-based ego and become, after 25 years, a triathlete. I hired a coach. I let go of a little of my bike speed and concentrated on my swim and run. I scored my first podium. Then my first age-group and masters wins. I started thinking about an Ironman again. I scored another age-group win. I suffered no injuries whatsoever.

Then, in my season finale, a total meltdown. Cramps up to my earlobes. Abject humiliation.

For about a minute. Maybe 90 seconds. I didn't have time for more than that. I had my first marathon coming up in a month.

God, I love this sport.

---

13 Not to spoil the surprise, but it turns out I didn't.
14 Besides my special moment with Walter Mondale.
15 *Frazz*, distributed by United Feature Syndicate. It's about an elementary school janitor who's kind of cool, kind of smart, and—I'm not sure how this happened— races triathlons.
16 Same wife the whole time!
17 Whereas, when working for someone else, merely irresponsible.
18 And riding like a guy who's got a race the next day just as often.
19 And should.

CHAPTER 3

Your Future in a Sport You Can Do for the Rest of Your Life

WHAT TO DO

An aspiring cyclist asked the great Eddy Merckx if there might be a formula for racing a bike so well. Merckx thought a moment and responded, "Just do it." Though not in those exact words. Supposedly what he said was, "Ride your bike, ride your bike, ride your bike." Although some accounts have him saying a little more concisely, "Ride your bike," or the elegant compromise, "Ride your bike. Lots." Or perhaps, *"Kar uw fiets. Dikwijls."* Or *"Ride la vostra bicicletta. Domande."* It seems only slightly more odd that a Belgian should say it in Italian than in English, especially since the line is also attributed to Fausto Coppi and God knows how many other bike racers (you might just as well try to attribute "Preheat your oven to 325 degrees" to Julia Child) before Nike refined the sentiment into the simpler and more universal "Just do it" in 1988, with an initial advertising budget of 20 million reasons never to get the phrase wrong or attribute it to the wrong guy.

What I'm saying is, the simplest things can be so complicated, and vice versa.

Obviously, racing triathlons is not as simple as "Ride your bike, ride your bike, ride your bike."[1] And, with all due respect to Nike, "Just do it" is about as appropriate to triathlon as it is to bomb defusing. *Just doing* a 10K is to risk misery and injury.[2] *Just doing* a bicycle ride on a public road is to risk a poorly timed swerve amid lethally swift projectiles piloted by drivers a bit too concerned with keeping the special sauce off the cell phone. *Just doing* an open-water swim is to risk being eaten by Monstro the Whale.[3]

That's all right. If it's true that anything worth doing is worth doing the hard way, then maybe the hard way is the source of the worth. People don't seem to get quite the same joy out of falling asleep in front of the television with Cheez Doodles dust staining their fingertips as they do from harder things like triathlons.

What those people do get joy out of, though, is teasing athletes who falter.[4] If you still need a motive to do this right, you won't find a better one than those guys.

The first thing you're going to want to do is tell people about it. Tell your friends, tell your family, tell the spongy guy in the finance department with the orange fingers. Tell them now. Go on. Put the book down. I'll wait. Tell them you're going to do a triathlon, and tell them before you have a chance to think too much about it. You're setting yourself up to do something great, and I have, right here, the Formula for Greatness:[5]

Ignorance + Desperation = Greatness

Ignorance and desperation are the driving forces behind my proudest accomplishments. Some achievements take so much work that no informed person would take them on, and they grow into an irredeemable mess that no dignified person would bail on. Start dumb and grow into a lack of options, I say; then fall face first into the rewards.

So, seriously. Let the cat out of the bag and get going. Everybody will find out soon enough anyway when you have to explain the weight loss. Or the altered credit rating.

---

1   Right off the bat, Merckx (Coppi, whoever) left out a couple of sports, though you have to give him credit for having the foresight to repeat the phrase the correct number of times.
2   And a profound inability to quit telling your coworkers about it, followed by a swift and enduring return to the sofa.
3   If the dangers of open-water swimming aren't apparent enough without explanation, then I'm sorry: Hyperbole is in order.
4   The word is "schadenfreude." It means taking pleasure in the misfortunes of others. Its roots are from the German *Schaden*, meaning damage, and *Freude*, meaning joy. The *asshole* is silent.
5   How about that? You bought a CEO business book at a sports-book price! You're reaping the benefits of triathlon already.

Which brings us to: Go shopping. Triathlon isn't expensive,[6] but it isn't free. You'll need a certain amount of equipment, and you'll need someplace to swim. You'll need a coach or a book[7] because you'll need a training plan. You'll need to replace some calories. You'll need to fix equipment that breaks or wears out. You'll need to have those pants taken in.

But the first thing you need to go shopping for is a triathlon itself. Training without a race to aim for is like being engaged without a wedding date. Or a fiancée. You want to know what kind of race you're getting involved with, or you won't be able to train and even shop the right way. Logic would say, maybe, start with a sprint.[8] If you're not coming into the sport with a background in other endurance sports, it's smart to get the experience first and then see about adding mileage later. If you *are* coming into it with a background in other endurance sports, then starting with a sprint can make even more sense.[9] It's one thing to have an overachiever's personality; it's another yet to have the firepower to indulge it.

Still, the choice is there, and it's yours to make. I've seen an alarming number of beginners choose a half- or even full Ironman for their first race. In some cases, it makes sense[10] even if it doesn't exude wisdom. But in every other case, I don't get it. Ego? Pfft. To rip off yet another great work of literature,[11] a triathlon's a triathlon no matter how small.

---

6   It isn't. Excessively large houses are expensive. Luxury and high-performance cars are expensive. Chest pains are expensive. Money itself is expensive when you borrow it. Triathlon stuff can add up, but when you put it into that kind of perspective, it looks a little better. And believe me, triathletes put it into that kind of perspective all the time. "Well, I'm not spending it at the bar" and "I'm not blowing it on cigarettes" are rationalizations popularly voiced en route to the bike shops of America, largely by people who have never been tempted by smoky bars, anyway. Which, I guess, is the salient point.

7   Don't even think that this one is going to be sufficient.

8   This is how logic gets its reputation for being so . . . logical.

9   When I was a kid, there was a TV show called *The Six Million Dollar Man* about a test pilot with a bad airplane and an awesome insurance plan. He "touched asphalt," as the bike racers put it, wrecked his plane, and awoke from surgery with some pretty zoot replacement parts that made no sense to my 11-year-old, standard-issue brain. He was forever lifting and heaving heavy things and bad guys with one bionic arm (fine) and the same carbon-based spine he started out with (now, wait a minute). If there wasn't a sequel called *The Twelve Million Dollar Orthopedic Surgeon*, there should have been. My point: You bike yourself a pair of Ironman lungs, mind the 5K Fun Run bones in your feet.

10 Veterans of multiple marathons, say, who have a history of recreational cycling and swimming and *six frigging months to live*.

11 *Horton Hears a Who*, by Dr. Seuss. Duh.

WHAT TO EXPECT

I was out for a run in New York City—running being one of the best ways to explore a place, for my money—and turned down a canyon of old East Village tenement buildings into what was apparently Premonition Row. Up and down the uneven sidewalks, most of the street-level flats housed storefront psychics. Fortune-tellers. The shops looked pretty much the same until I came to the one with all the fire damage. And I had to stop. I couldn't run straight and handle the question at the same time: Didn't anybody see it coming?

Maybe the seers just knew better than to look. Maybe, like the tee-totaling bartender, they knew the dangers of their own product only too well. After all, if you knew the future, you'd just want to change it, and if you could change it, then it would no longer be the future you took great pains to see. Worse yet, what if you could see the future and do nothing but wait? I had to walk while I sorted it out. I could just see myself striding, deep in thought, into the grille of a taxi. Which didn't happen, complicating the puzzle further yet.

From what I can see, the frightening thing about the future is not that it might be ominous but that it's probably mundane.[1]

But I can't see much. Sometimes I'm glad of that—what would be the point of racing[2] if the outcome were predetermined and posted? Other times,[3] I confess it would be nice to have a peek.

How about a compromise? You're a human being; you deserve uncertainty. You're a triathlete; you deserve some clue to what the sport has in store for you. You paid $21.95[4] for this book, so you surely deserve something.

The nice thing about the future is that it's usually somebody else's past. Maybe my triathlon past looks a little like your triathlon future.[5]

You know how Dickens starts *A Tale of Two Cities*? Yes, you do, even if you don't think you do. It's all over the place. He writes, "It was the best of times, it was the worst of times." Triathlon can be a lot like that, only without all the beheadings.[6]

Triathlon is the best of times: What is more joyful than motion for motion's sake? The loose dog runs. That little kid in *The Family Circus* repeats the crooked-dotted-line gag every eight weeks or so. Chuck Berry sang about "No Particular Place to Go." Triathlon is that joy of motion with three options.

Three options, it should be emphasized, that can be done in some beautiful surroundings.[7] I have swum across the Straits of Mackinac; I

---

1   Most of the time, it just turns out to be the same thing as the present, only it happens a little later. I guess that's why they put it there, where you can't see it, so the suspense can make it a little more intriguing.

2   Racing? Hell, life.

3   I don't mean times like when investing in stocks, though I suppose that would be handy. I mean times like running with Nils. Nils is fantastic to run with. He and I are of similar ability. He's bright and enthusiastic and talks a lot about interesting things, and he chooses swell places to run. But sometimes Nils knows where the run ends, and I don't, and for the latter portions of those runs, or what I assume, hope, or pray to be the latter portions, Nils enjoys a serenity that is so profoundly missing from my own fatigued and impossible-to-pace life that I would hit the afterburners, surge ahead, ditch his happy pants, and leave him to enjoy his nirvana by himself if I only knew what he knew—that is, how to get home and how much more of a dwindling energy supply is needed to get there.

4   Plus tax.

5   And if it involves a chance to run with Nils, go for it in spite of what I told you in note 3.

6   *A Tale of Two Cities* is about the French Revolution. Nothing like 10 years of guillotinings to put a two-minute drafting penalty into perspective.

7   Not to mention exclusive surroundings. I like nice real estate, but I'm not terribly inclined to pay enough money for a house that I feel some sort of obligation to stay inside in order to get my money's worth. Might just as well wander through nice neighborhoods—location, location, location, they say—and enjoy the sights,

have run the streets of Manhattan. I bicycled home from my newspaper job on September 12, 2001, taking the long way home because routine had lost its ability to comfort, pedaling through a stillness and numbness that would have seemed postapocalyptic had the word not, in 36 hours, become cliché. I rode past hay fields gone from last week's amber to the same drab beige as everything else until a pair of sandhill cranes stood to

the history, and the atmosphere while somebody else stays inside and writes the mortgage check. The problem is, one of the things those people see themselves paying for is the right not to share their neighborhood with outsiders. Pull on a pair of running shoes, though, and you can enjoy their roads all you want; they don't know you don't live there. And really, what kind of threat do you pose running around in what amounts to lingerie with a sports-gear logo? (NB: This sort of tourism works best while running. Bikes go a little too fast to safely operate while rubbernecking, and swimming in their pools really would violate the whole premise.)

their full height and, in slow-motion unison, wing to six-foot wing, lifted off into the empty sky. For once I could see the future, and it was going to be all right.

Triathlon is the worst of times: I gave freedom a task; I took motion for motion's sake and assigned it a destination and a deadline. I learned to burn off stress, and then I turned around and courted it. There was another race to finish, a personal record to break, or a placing to pursue so that I might qualify for an event even farther away, more expensive, and more stressful. I trained in the cold and wet and in fading light. I listened to motorists' suggestions of alternative venues.[8] I tested my coworkers' and my wife's patience with yawns in the morning, restless legs in bed, an obnoxious appetite, and a self-righteousness that was of their manufacture, not mine, but nonetheless made their French fries half as satisfying in my presence.

The best times and the worst grew in intensity but took on familiarity. They would burn more and sting less. I'd score some form of triumph—anything from a masters division win to sticking with a miserable interval workout when nobody was there to see if I quit—I'd raise my arms, and by the time they fell to my sides I'd be picking the victory apart, seeing where to improve. Good wasn't good enough. It must have seemed to others like pathological dissatisfaction, but it felt like the definition of satisfaction. Conversely, there was comfort in the repetition of defeats—the final-stretch meltdowns, the bad luck, the bad days. The more bad days you have, the more you survive. The more you survive, the less you dread. "Oh, no" becomes "Oh, this again."

Can you see your future better the more you cram into your past? Or does your future become less certain as you fill it with more options? Is there really any difference between the best and worst of times?

It's 2004 in Italy, not 1794 in France, but it's the best of times and the worst of times again. I've spent a chilly spring morning riding my bike with two friends from the States; with Paolo, a former national cham-

---

8   The waterfront off Olive Park in Chicago is nicknamed Tri-Geek Beach. It's separated from Lake Michigan's waves by a breakwater and from Chicago's cement by a steel seawall with markers painted on it at a quarter and a half mile. It couldn't be more ideal, and a smart visiting tri-geek would have left it at that. But I listened to a helpful tip from someone who looked reliable. "Swim past the second marker to the end of the seawall," he said, "and the round-trip is a perfect half-Ironman 1.2 miles." What he didn't say was that the Shore Patrol didn't share his view of where the swim zone ended, and my next helpful tip of the day came from a boat and through a bullhorn. Now, the taunt is little more than white noise to cyclists, and runners hear it plenty as well. But it takes some doing to get yelled at to use the sidewalk while you're swimming. I'm so proud.

pion from Milan; and with a dozen brand-new friends in last year's race kit. They are impressed with Paolo and not sure about the Americans, but they're gathering information. We're on the upward slope of a mountain outside Vinci, and we're flying. Everything hurts. The cool air feels caustic in my throat. Blood is coursing through me like the Gauley River, but it's pushing more toxins than the Houston Ship Channel. I need to see the future badly because it seems important to know where the top of the mountain is in order to predict whether I have any chance at all of arriving there with the five remaining Italians I'm trying to hang with. It's not an unreasonable wish, it turns out. I'd like to think I laid out everything I had before I drifted off the back, cross-eyed, and that it wouldn't have mattered even if I had known that the road would level off in 50 m. But I didn't know.

I also didn't know why they were stopping. But they leaned their bikes against an iron fence, and when we were all back together, they gestured toward the little summit café and we went in. I didn't even know I liked coffee. I never liked it before. I've liked it ever since.

We went back outside and leaned on the fence where we'd propped our bikes. I looked out over the valley. Maybe the fog had lifted. Maybe I was just seeing especially clearly. But I could see where I was, and I was at one of those moments when every ride I'd ever done, every cramp, every bonk, every wave of nausea—hell, every bad day I'd ever had and any rotten one that was on its way—had propped me on that fence rail at that moment, and it struck me as a pretty good deal.

The best of times? The worst of times? They're exactly that: times. Time is a vehicle. It doesn't judge, reward, punish, vindicate, or heal all wounds; it just moves you from one moment to another. This sport takes a lot of time. It yields a lot of moments.

You could do worse for a future.

HOW TO EXPLAIN IT

've long since lost track of how many triathlons I've competed in,[1] but I can tell you exactly how many I've watched: zippo.

That's not to say that triathlons aren't good for spectators. They're wonderful to watch. I just prefer to watch them from within, as a competitor or a volunteer. One of the great joys of triathlon is that you *can* watch them that way, racing—or at least sharing the course—with the elites. You can't do that with professional football or auto racing,[2] which

---

1   This has more to do with my personality than any vast wealth of experience; I couldn't tell you how many tetanus shots I've had, either.

2   Playing catch in the stadium parking lot notwithstanding, and driving around with an "I ain't speedin,' I'm qualifyin'" sticker on your rear window between the number sticker and the counterfeit whizzing-Calvin sticker most certainly notwithstanding.

just happen to be two of the most popular spectator sports in America.[3] Nor, given those sports' certainty of concussions and collisions, would you necessarily want to, which completes a certain circular logic. As our mothers explained to us when we were young, carnage is for watching.

Speaking of circular logic and explanations, if you're going to be doing triathlons, then you're going to be doing some explaining. Spectator sports have analysts and announcers to explain intricacies and fill down-time. Understanding begets interest. That's why, say, a baseball game can move along like a tortoise with tendinitis and still be positively scintillating.[4] Your friends watching you train and race don't have that network of analysts. They have you.

But you have me. Together we can anticipate some of their questions. And if we miss a few, well, so do the football analysts.[5]

Q: First question: Why?

A: Why not?

Q: Because it looks like it hurts.

A: It sort of hurts, yes.

Q: You actually enjoy pain?

A: No one likes pain. But too much comfort never got anybody very far, either.

Q: That sounded just a little pompous.

A: If I am pompous, it won't last long. Any fool can suffer pain, but pain doesn't suffer fools. If I've developed a tolerance for buckets of pain and I'm a little smug about it, I'm just a teaspoon away from having my boat swamped. I consider this to be good. Like it or not, pain is one of the things that make us human. I know other creatures can feel pain;[6] I'm not sure they do much more than react to it. Maybe they anticipate and avoid it to some extent. I seriously doubt that they court it and measure it and experiment with it the way we humans do.[7] Pain is information— good information, even poetry, that happens to have a grating voice,[8]

---

3   Advocates of each sport, and any number of other sports, will tell you theirs is the top spectator sport and back it up with authentic but curiously nonparallel statistics, proving only that the number-one participant sport in America is arguing about the number-one spectator sport.

4   I'm told.

5   No one has yet explained to my satisfaction why a team will pay a place kicker $1.5 million a year and then put a big net behind the goalpost so the $90 ball doesn't end up in the $60 seats.

6   I have four cats, and I have stepped on tails. I have heard expressions of pain too descriptive for language.

7   It says something that we're the only species to have purchased 57 million Bob Dylan albums.

8   I'm telling you, pain is Bob Dylan.

and you're robbing yourself if you don't learn an appreciation for it. How peculiar that we've built a modern lifestyle on distractions and conveniences and layers of insulation between ourselves and discomfort, yet we feel less alive and individual than ever. How ironic that the way not to feel like a number is to pin a big one to a race belt while volunteers with Magic Markers draw digits onto your shoulders and legs.

Q: Good Lord.

A: Sorry. It's easy to get philosophical.

Q: I mean, good Lord, they draw numbers on you with Magic Markers?

A: It comes off easily with soap, water, and a washcloth.[9]

Q: What's a race belt?

A: A light elastic belt with a quick buckle for you to attach your race number to. Hardly any races require you to pin a number on for the swim,

---

9   If you use enough sunscreen, they come off before the race even starts.

and usually you don't have to ride with a bib flapping in the wind as long as you've got a number visible on your bike. So you attach it to a belt and put it on for the run.

Q: Don't you wear some kind of electronic timing thing?

A: We do use timing chips. Those are why everybody in the race is wearing an ankle band and why you hear all that beeping as racers run across the red sensor mats at the entrances and exits to the transition zone. With the chip, you get accurate splits and same-day results. They're great.

Q: So why bother with all the numbers on your arms and legs, your bike, your swim cap, and your race belt?

A: The electronic chips are great, but they're not foolproof. Sometimes people lose them in the water or peel them off with their wetsuits. Sometimes one just doesn't work—it's an electronic device, after all.[10] The traditionally displayed numbers also allow officials to identify racers. Likewise, race photographers find them invaluable for organizing and selling their wares. They're tradition, too, part of the image. And they're one more tool for the volunteers guarding your gear.[11]

Q: And for the sheriff's department dive team.

A: The very bored sheriff's department dive team. Although it's possible to die during a triathlon,[12] it rarely happens. A 2008 *New York Times* story noted just 23 deaths during triathlons over the previous four years and hundreds of thousands of racers, making triathlon marginally more risky than navel gazing, a good deal safer than skipping a dentist's appointment,[13] and more or less equal in risk to discovering an invoice around the house that shows your husband has purchased a "Speedo Comfort Thong."

Q: A thong? Are you *serious*?

A: That's exactly the tone of voice my wife used. They were sandals. Flip-flops.

Q: That's good to know. What do you wear to race in?

A: The dress code is pretty relaxed. You can wear whatever is comfortable as long as it doesn't violate local decency ordinances.[14] The standard wardrobe has evolved into a skintight, quick-drying, one- or two-piece

---

10   Pardon me a moment while I indulge a sudden need to back up my files.

11   Anybody who wants to steal your bike has to steal your number belt and a Magic Marker first, and criminals just aren't that ambitious.

12   And impossible not to think about it while reading the thorough and creatively morbid liability release form.

13   Or driving to a dentist's appointment. How's that for doomed?

14   And by "local," I still seem at times to mean local to a Florida beach frequented by middle-aged German tourists.

affair that's kind of a tank top with a zipper and nominally padded bike shorts that can be worn start to finish.[15] Women seem just as likely to race in a swimsuit. But you'll see people in running shorts, too, and loose t-shirts. You can hardly blame someone who prefers a little space between skin and fabric.

Q: Are there changing rooms?

A: Sometimes there are changing tents in the longer races. But most of the time you just wear something that dries quickly.

Q: Those longer races: How do you, ah . . .

A: Everybody asks that. One answer, again, involves quick-drying fabric. Not everyone has the same level of pragmatic shamelessness,[16] though, and there are facilities along the course.

Q: Bike racers shave their legs so they can clean up better after a crash, right? Do triathletes crash a lot?

---

15   Design the same ensemble with wide red and white horizontal stripes and wear it with a handlebar mustache and a straw boater hat, and you wouldn't be out of place at a nineteenth-century beach party in the Hamptons.

16   Or the shoe budget, if you catch my drift.

A: No. But a lot of us used to race bikes, and we all figured out that our legs felt better, looked better, and lotioned up better without hair all over them. The volunteers with the Magic Markers seem to appreciate it, too.

Q: Whatever. Can you swim with water wings?

A: No. But you can swim with a wetsuit,[17] and that's even better. Not only does neoprene float, but the wetsuit manufacturers know which part of the suit should float the most, so it helps the more marginal swimmers stay more streamlined and use better form. You swim faster in a wetsuit.

Q: Doesn't that make the better swimmers mad?

A: They're wearing them, too, and they're way ahead of the rest of us, regardless.

Q: What's the best way to watch a triathlon, then?

A: If you're there to watch me, bring a magazine. I could be gone a while. But bring a magazine you don't mind ditching because I'm hardly the most interesting thing going on. If we're swimming in a big lake, you're probably in a park, which isn't a bad place to wander around, race or no race. And the other competitors are pretty interesting, too. Watch the first racers come out of the water shoulder to shoulder and head for their bikes, doing a neoprene striptease at full gallop. Watch them whip through the transition zone like a shoplifter in a convenience store. Watch them go, but don't follow them. Head back to the waterfront and watch the others come out, head in, and shoot through. Every racer has her own pace, his own style, her own motives, and his own story. Some swim at full throttle to get an early lead. Others look like they're warming up. Watch the really efficient swimmers, the ones who have figured out how to travel half again as far with each armful of water. She looks like she's loafing through a warm-up *and* getting herself a head start. Watch guys like me veer off course; watch the always terrific lifeguards bring us back in like cutting ponies: *Yo, git along, little dogie.* Only a few minutes after the leaders touch bottom and leapfrog through the shallows, watch people wade ashore like shipwreck victims. There are wide smiles; the crux is behind them. There are second thoughts; more racing ahead than fuel in the tank. Everybody has a story.

Q: By now you're out on your bike, right? Can I get in the car and cheer for you out on the course?

---

17   Within limits. Sooner or later you'll hear the term "wetsuit legal" around the registration area. If the water temperature is 78 degrees Fahrenheit or below, the race is wetsuit legal; racers can squeeze into the rubber. From 79 to 83 degrees, you can wear a wetsuit if you want. You won't be eligible for awards, but if it helps you finish and makes you feel safe, they're not going to stop you. Once the water temperature reaches 84, they're not allowed at all. The middle of a lake is not a place where you want to get overheated and woozy.

A: That's a great thought but a bad idea. If you can even get to your car, you'll likely have to go through or near the same bottleneck the triathletes are taking their bikes through. Out on the road, the congestion eases a little, but the speeds and risks ramp up dramatically. Let the riders have the road. Hang out by the transition zone and watch them come back home. You might not see the same relief you saw in some of the swimmers, but you'll see an even wider range of fatigue and self-analysis as people consider how well they've set themselves up for their run. Brains can be operating at less than peak capacity at this point, and, without being too mean about it, there is potential for comedy. You will see creative steering and dismounts. You will feel much better about the time you lost your car in the mall parking lot. You will see socks that somehow take five, even ten minutes to put on successfully.

Q: Is this the part where a few people try to run with their helmets still on?

A: It is. And it's the part where people will actually twist around and look to see whose lower body they've been assigned for the day.

Q: Do I ever get to see you out on the course?

A: Sure. There may be shortcuts to different parts of the course. You might feel inspired to take a bit of a walk. In some cases, you might be able to get around on a bike, but check ahead. The last thing you want is to get in someone's way. In fact, the last thing you *do* could be to get in someone's way if you push your luck running across the road on the bike course. Put it this way: The racers have other things on their minds besides watching for spectators, and, right or wrong, they believe the course is clear. Now put it this way: If cyclists can be seriously hurt or killed hitting an object—and they can—then so can you, the object. And you're not wearing a helmet.

Q: Can I cheer for people I don't know?

A: Absolutely. The racers soak up that energy.[18] You know who else to cheer for? The volunteers and the cops.

Q: I imagine the scene around the finish line is pretty cool.

A: It really is.[19] And don't feel bad if you miss the winners. The real drama is midpack and back. That's where doubts vanish, where limits are reached, where oaths sworn are replaced with vows renewed. The

---

18 We even know the code. If we hear reports of how far behind the leader we are, we're having a very good day. Shouts of "Looking good, looking good" sound good, sound good. Reassurances like "You're almost there; you can do it" are welcome and appreciated but not a good sign.

19 Fifty yards beyond, not so cool. That's where the throwing up tends to take place.

finish line is where people become things for the first time:[20] winners. Finishers. Triathletes. It's where they leave old selves behind: smokers. Heavyweights. Quitters. But be careful. The energy is poorly contained. You might feel the beginnings of a transformation yourself. From skeptical to tempted.

Q: Me?

A: You.

Q: Why?

A: . . .

Q: Why not?

---

20 Making the finish line the most inappropriately named place since Greenland. Or any town in the Midwest that begins with the word "Mount."

CHAPTER 1

Training Day

THE TIME

I n the spring of 2008, about the time our most recent iteration of a Gilded Age finished its crosswind base leg and lined up for its final approach,[1] the Swiss watch company Romain Jerome introduced a groundbreaking new timepiece, the ultimate in luxury and exclusivity: a $300,000 watch that does not tell you what time it is.

The idea, in those heady days, was that any old billionaire could spend $300,000 on a watch. But it took a very special[2] billionaire to *waste* $300,000 on a watch. Romain Jerome didn't quite put it in those

---

1 In the sense that Wile E. Coyote is lining up for the final approach after he runs off the edge of the cliff but before he looks down.

2 One of the signature traits of a Romain Jerome watch is what RJ calls its "Titanic DNA." What RJ means in less flowery terms is that the watches are made with steel from the sunken corpse of the famous luxury liner. So when I say "special," what I mean in less flowery terms is "infinitely creepy."

words, but the gist was the same. As CEO Yvan Arpa[3] explained it to the *Wall Street Journal*,[4] most people feel that time is the ultimate luxury; ergo, if you have so much time that you can afford to ignore it, you're very rich indeed.

It's interesting to see all these capitalist tools get so excited about time, that most socialist of currencies. Nothing is more equally granted than time; it's doled out to everybody at the rate of 60 minutes per hour. No inheritance, no dividends, no bonuses. No bargaining. Everybody gets the same wages, direct deposit. You. Me. Yvan Arpa and Romain Jerome and their customers. With all due respect[5] to those guys, I'm not looking for a way to conspicuously ignore my share.

I want a way to beat the system.

Which brings us back to triathlon. We triathletes twist time like a pipe cleaner in a blender. A few hundred of us show up at a race and cover the exact same distance[6] in a few hundred different amounts of time and we all go home with the same t-shirt and the same medal, and some of us finish in less time than we predicted and some of us finish in more time than we planned, and people who finish in more time than they hoped get done before someone who finished in less time than he or she expected and they all start at the beginning and finish at the end, and a race is its own lifetime and time is just the string that holds it together and you don't need a $300,000 watch to tell you that time is not exactly concrete.

Darn good thing, too, because concrete, linear time wouldn't serve a triathlete well. We need too much of it, the way we train and travel and obsess. So we bend time some more—double it back and use it twice. Tie it in knots.

Einstein said that if you travel faster than the speed of light, time reverses itself, but it's not worth the jet lag.[7] Einstein didn't mention triathlon specifically,[8] but there's something about self-propelled forward motion at any speed that seems to have the same effect. Specifically, when thrown into the context of a busy life, an hour of training doesn't take 60 minutes. Well, maybe it does, but then whatever else you do during the

---

3   The preacher.

4   The choir loft.

5   Which, if they thought the watch was going to buy them some, there's 300 large down the drain.

6   Give or take a few detours in the lake for those of us who may not lift our heads out of the water for a peek quite often enough.

7   Also the airsickness bag. Talk about a device you don't want working in reverse.

8   Though he seemed to have the right idea about it. He did mention that "life is like riding a bicycle. To keep your balance you must keep moving," summing up in two lines what I'm trying to squeeze into a whole book. Guess we know who's the genius.

day bucks the formula. You become more efficient. You don't become as profoundly fatigued as quickly. You sleep better at night. You think more clearly during the day.

I know what you're thinking, or at least what your coworkers are thinking: It all sounds like a big, fat rationalization. I suspect so myself sometimes. But life encourages us to conduct occasional tests. Things get out of hand. There's too much to do, and there's too little time. Something must give, and sometimes it's training. So you give up that hour or two, or three, of training and . . . discover at the end of the day that you've accomplished the same amount of stuff. Or less. What gives?

This may come as a surprise in a three-in-one sport like triathlon, but one thing we don't do is multitask. Remember, we swim, *then* bike, *then* run—one at a time. Trying to combine the activities may or may not be against the rules,[9] but it doesn't speed things up.[10] Experts tell us that multitasking in daily life doesn't work, either. Often they tell us on the radio, knowing full well we're not sitting around staring into the speaker like Howdy Doody listening to the Lone Ranger, but that doesn't blow the theory. It just means nothing is absolute.[11] You have to use some sense. Bike commuting, for example, is terrific multitasking. Swim commuting, not so much.

The real value of triathlon training may lie in its total contrast with multitasking, the way it strips your existence down to a single focused task. I get asked a lot if, as a writer and a cartoonist, I come up with ideas while I'm working out.[12] It's not unreasonable to think I might, but it would be incorrect. I don't write at all when I run, swim, or ride. But I write a whole

---

9   At any rate, it doesn't come up a lot in the pre-race briefings.

10   Not that I haven't seen it tried. I was working a half-marathon as a bike marshal, riding alongside the lead pack of runners to keep them from making any wrong turns. It was easy work, since the race followed the only road, which in turn followed a lakeshore. But as it happened, the race also followed a night of heavy thunderstorms. One section of the road dipped a little low where the lake ran a little high, and the pack bunched up as runners tried to pick their way through half a foot of murky water. Front-of-the-pack runners are not, by nature, terribly patient, and it wasn't an orderly queue. Runners ran wide, forgetting that while water may seek its own level, dirt is a little more content to, say, drop about five feet straight down off the shoulder of the road. It was like watching reverse Whack-a-Mole as runners popped downward, fully upright but with eyes suddenly at ankle level. I don't know if any of them went on to win the race, but I can assure you that none of the swimmer-runners pulled ahead of the guys who stuck to running.

11   But not absolutely nothing.

12   Odd that one of the guys I run with is a gastroenterologist, and no one asks him if he performs sigmoidoscopies during, ah, workouts (scrambling desperately here to avoid using the word "runs." Damn. Sorry).

lot better afterward. I have no doubt there's a physical aspect to it, the whole sound-mind-in-a-sound-body construct. Freshly oxygenated blood flowing in copious quantities is bound to rinse through the gray matter, and it's hard to see anything but benefits coming from that.

But I believe the true value of training lies in its monotony. In a world of a thousand distractions,[13] there's something soothing about hav-

---

13   And a book of a thousand footnotes.

ing your attention trimmed to a single entity, and you can't do better than one that involves a cyclic motion over an extended time in a largely straight line. You focus on the horizon. Your limbs carve out a rhythm while your breath harmonizes and your pulse holds it together in this odd visceral jazz that vibes concentration.[14] Your hard drive is defragmenting. You are doing something dangerously close to meditation, a mantra in motion.[15] Maybe you're feeling that runner's high people[16] keep bringing up, and that's why you return to the real world with more time than you had when you left, feeling like some kind of Einstein.

Or maybe all you did was find something that's more interesting than television, and if you're the average American, there's an extra 30 hours a week right there.

We triathletes, we've beat the system. We get more done by adding training to our day. We bend time by using it in a straight line. We burn energy playing and return to work with more. We buy watches that record a hundred laps with accuracy to a hundredth of a second and worry about the fleeting nature of life far less than the guy with the $300,000 watch that doesn't tell time.

It's not logical, but it makes sense. To someone. In 2009, Romain Jerome introduced a follow-up to that watch. It's essentially the same thing, but with one difference: This one tells time.

It's selling quite well.

---

14   Craaaaazy, man.

15   I wouldn't go around calling it that, though. Or shouldn't have, once. I was 10 miles from home, pondering a flat tire and newly limited options, when an evangelist in a silver sedan offered me a ride and a sermon. Having already learned about the limitations of self-patching tire sealants on my own, I learned about the limitations of the athlete's spiritual life from her. "Do not glorify your body at your soul's cost," she chided. I was grateful for the ride and tried to repay her with some reassurances. I thought maybe I'd explain how standing in the ditch, staring at a disabled bike, scratching my ass through a skintight, brightly colored montage of sponsor logos hadn't felt especially glorious, but I chose to accentuate the positive. I left out the jazz metaphor (jazz musicians sometimes smoke marijuana, you understand), but I did explain the focus, the horizon, the rhythm, and the repetition. I was on a roll until "mantra." Turns out certain evangelists don't go for mantra. Should have used the jazz metaphor after all.

16   Mostly people who don't run. It's very odd.

THE EFFORT

My father was a music teacher, and he's still a Methodist. Because of the former, he moonlighted. Because of the latter, he moonlighted as a church choir director. Because of the combination, I spent a lot of my youth inside buildings[1] hearing about the importance of hard work.

Whether your aim was to get a good job or to get into heaven, the sermon was the lesson, and the equation was the same: Effort translates directly to success.

What a lazy thing to say.

In the Church and University of the Almighty Triathlon, the truth is shown to be a little more complicated. When I close in on the finish

---

1   Buildings with fluorescent lights. Thank the Protestant gods (that would be God, I guess, wouldn't it?) for Vitamin D–fortified milk or I'd have died of rickets. To this day, I cannot wear white cycling shorts because I look too much like I'm riding around pantsless.

line, all flushed and woozy and thoroughly drained, I can count on seeing people still rolling into the transition zone on their bikes. On their bikes! They look just as drained as I feel, and they've still got the entire run course to go. And it's only getting hotter. These guys are *tough*.

In the strictest, most nearsighted interpretation of success,[2] am I the more successful racer because I'm finishing sooner? If that's the case, then why, in the strictest and most nearsighted interpretation of effort, am I not working as hard? Or working just as hard but not as long? It doesn't fit.

The work-ethic authorities have an explanation: Maybe I didn't put as much work into the race as the guys behind me, but that's only because I clearly put more work into *preparing* for the race during the days, weeks, and years beforehand. Well. Maybe I did, maybe I didn't. I'm not saying there's no correlation. I'm saying it's complicated. And it should be. In an uncomplicated world, triathlons would be conducted on treadmills and ergometers, and finishers would be sorted not by minutes and seconds but by calories or kilojoules, and even Wednesday-night church-choir practices would seem positively engaging by comparison.[3]

The teachers and the preachers talk about work as if it were input, but scientists measure it in terms of output. I think the scientists are the closest to the mark and that the truth lies in what's almost a footnote. They say that

$$W = F \times D$$

Work (W) equals the force (F) applied to an object times the distance (D) that object moves in the direction of the force applied. Dig that part at the end: *in the direction of the force applied.* You can wear yourself out pushing on the door marked "pull," and you haven't, as far as the scientist is concerned, done any work at all.[4]

You want to race, you have to train. The rest is just details. It couldn't be simpler.

---

2   As always seems to be the case, two strict interpretations create a whole lot of vague. Black plus white equals a vast sea of gray, after all. In school, I was told work was a means to an end: a diploma, a job, a promotion, wealth. In church, work was promoted as its own reward. My wife used to have a t-shirt that said, "Jesus Is Coming! Look Busy," which pretty much summed up the whole Protestant work ethic as far as I could see, though neither the Protestants nor the t-shirt people would like to think so.

3   I know of what I speak.

4   This has uncomfortable implications for a writer who might, say, blow seven paragraphs writing a chapter on work without yet getting to anything resembling a point. Perhaps some focus is in order.

But it could be infinitely more complicated. I could tell you, right here, how to train for a triathlon, like a thousand other books, magazine articles, and Web sites that dispense copious and, over time, seemingly equal amounts of common sense and voodoo and timelessness and fads and trends and ongoing experiments. I won't, though. I haven't given you a directly applicable morsel of information yet,[5] and I'm not about to start now. W = F x D covers the essence, anyway. God is in the details.[6] Me, I'm here for the stories.

Essence: Your body will only give you in competition what you ask of it in training.

Details: No details. The logic is unassailable.

Stories: I learned this lesson between my first and second bicycle races. I had spent much of my youth riding at one consistent, fairly intense level of effort. Imagine my surprise when I learned that bike races didn't take place at that level of effort. They went much easier or much, *much* harder, and once you failed to keep up with the hard part,[7] you were done for the day. The problem was easy enough to identify, but there were not a lot of solutions in the form of books and research on bicycle racing and training to be had in early-1980s rural America. So I made something up. Foreshadowing my multisport future, I recalled "enduros." My junior varsity football coach called them enduros, anyway. Exercise physiologists call them intervals. Everybody on the team called them run-and-pukes, and I recalled them feeling a lot like that bike race did before I got dropped. So I found a low-traffic loop where I could take my bike and replicate the same on-again, off-again tunnel vision,[8] and I had at it for a few weeks before my next race. In a perfect world, the next sentence would say that I won that race in a lung-searing sprint. I didn't. I won it with a long breakaway, at the same damn speed I rode before all those intervals, after the pack let me go because most of them didn't know me from Adam and the rest of them just knew me as the novice who got

---

5   Which doesn't put me as far behind the books and articles and Web sites as we'd all like to think.

6   Commonly attributed to the architect Mies van der Rohe and the art historian Aby Warburg, though assumed without verification to have been first said by the writer Gustave Flaubert, who was quite possibly beaten to the phrase by Michelangelo; the variation "The devil is in the details" wouldn't appear until much later, and while unattributed, you can sure see where it came from.

7   Which commenced straight from the gun until the pack had safely burned off excess baggage like, well, me.

8   If you try this, I recommend lining up the crux of the "on" interval to go past Marie's house after she dumps you and before you get over it. That pretty much takes care of any temptation to ease off.

dropped. But if it weren't for the intervals, I wouldn't have been in the race long enough to sneak away.[9]

Essence: Actually, your body will give you a little more in competition than you asked of it in training.

Details: The moment you take that notion too much to heart, you're toast.

Stories: That's one of the reasons we compete. Roger Bannister didn't break the 4-minute mile in a practice,[10] after all. When we show up to compete, we're a little better prepared, a little more rested, a little more motivated, and a lot more surrounded by people. We're with people we want to beat, people we don't want to disappoint, and people with timers and clipboards and the power to enter our results into the permanent record. But more than that, we're surrounded by the unexpected, and we're drawn into efforts that we don't even know we're not supposed to be capable of. There's magic in competition. The key is to stay just shy of where the magic ends and reality returns because when reality does return, it's invariably pissed. I remember one race like that. I swam well, if not remarkably, but when I got on my bike I lit it up. I reeled in other riders like Lake Erie walleye[11] and felt great doing it. I floated up hills. I sliced through the wind. I shifted up. I shifted up again, and I didn't shift down. I sailed through transition and set out running on legs that had already forgiven and forgotten the bike effort. Briefly. The meltdown was instant and complete, like flipping a switch, and in the remaining 3 or 4 miles I squandered twice what I had gained during 28 miles of magic. I remember this race well because it *has taken place a good 8 or 10 times.*

Essence: Okay, so your body will only do in competition what you ask it to do in racing *and* competition.

Details: Just as human progress hinges on eureka[12] moments, athletic progress hinges on breakthroughs.

---

9   I'm sorry. If you want your stories wrapped up with a tidy bow, don't read nonfiction.

10   Though he didn't exactly break it at the world championships, either. He broke it at a diddly little local dual meet that was significant only in retrospect. Except to Bannister. To him, it loomed significant as his last chance to break the 4-minute mile before his rival John Landy had a chance to do it at a meet in Finland (where, in fact, Landy did; he ran the mile a second and a half faster but 46 days slower). So there's a certain now-or-never motivation that competition fosters as well.

11   Walleye are tasty but about as challenging as picking corn. Note the lack of acclaim for, or existence of, "The Old Man and the Walleye" or *Moby Walleye.*

12   Wow. Archimedes, of course, shouted that word running naked down the street straight from his bathtub, and I'm only now working him into a book about triathlon?

Stories: I don't know if those meltdowns repeat themselves because I'm an idiot or a genius, but it's almost always how my first race of the season goes, and it's just as nearly always followed by a terrific result. It's almost like it's a necessary crucible to get my season in gear, or a wall I have to run smack into before I can find the door, run through it, and get on with things. I sure hope not. Like the joke that never gets old,[13] the bad race never feels acceptable.

Essence: Your body may get a little too good at doing what it's asked to do in training.

Details: Don't get too comfortable. This problem can sneak up on you.

Stories: Today's athletes, including me, can use expensive electronic aids such as heart rate monitors and power meters to make an array of excuses that were previously unavailable. My equipment tells me that I can keep up with just about anybody,[14] but at approximately twice the heart rate,[15] meaning the effort is doomed to end in pain and sorrow.[16] For this, I blame years of commuting four miles to work under my own power. Four miles is just far enough to redline it the entire distance if you are, let's just say, chronically late to work. Unfortunately, most triathlons, bike races, and marathons last somewhat longer, and my endurance is not exactly what I'd like it to be. Then again, I may just be untalented.[17]

Essence: Actually, your body really doesn't respond to training the way you think it does.

Details: What your body responds to is rest.

Stories: I'm a great big sleep-deprived hypocrite for even mentioning this, but it's important enough for a do-as-I-say-not-as-I-do moment. What we think of as training, the kinetic, sweaty, fun part that makes you hungry, is only half the equation. With apologies for pretending I know anything about physiology, that's when you stress and damage tissues and systems. Sleep is when you rebuild those tissues and systems into something a little more deluxe. It goes beyond sleep, too. It's important to take a day off from hard training, or even training at all, once or even

---

13   "My dog has no nose!"
     "How does he smell?"
     "Awful!"
     That joke.
14   This is an egregious exaggeration.
15   This is a very minor exaggeration.
16   This is absolutely accurate.
17   Also, I run like I'm wearing a cup. For this, I blame enduros.

twice a week.[18] Training at the same intensity, day in, day out, is not much more than the long-term equivalent of the steady-state training that got my butt kicked in that first bike race. You need to go easy once in a while so you can really hit it hard the next day. Finally, a poorly rested body is a body that's about to be injured. And an injured body is a body that's looking at a whole bunch of rest days in a row, far more than even your highest estimates of how long it's going to take for that knot or twinge to go away.

---

18 The truth? If you live a normal life, with normal responsibilities, the world will force an adequate number of rest days on you, anyway. If not, you're either too high-strung, you have too much time on your hands, or you need to move out of your parents' basement.

Essence: Everything in moderation.

Details: Especially moderation in moderation.

Stories: Right. Exercise responsibly so that you've got the luxury of going on a real bender when it's time. And don't be so sure the bender will always take place on race day. Sometimes you end up training with someone who's going longer or faster than you planned and is worth sticking with anyway. Sometimes you can just tell you're primed for an epic. Sometimes you get lost. Sometimes—often—nature loves a good prank, be it fickle headwinds, gravity clusters,[19] or making you a little dumb in the first place. Embrace these festivals of suffering. They're the days you will remember, the ones that you'll tell and retell on long rides. Epics like my Arches run. I was a college student not majoring in geology but willing to play that role if it meant I could join a Geology Department field trip and finally see the canyons of the American West. It was a low-key sort of trip, all cars, granola, and sleeping bags over Thanksgiving break. We reached Arches National Monument[20] in exactly the kind of cold and darkness that a moonless November promises and the kind of dryness Utah promises. No tents necessary. When I woke up in the morning, I scrubbed the ice off my glasses and looked around at a scene that was as alien as it was gorgeous. Even the sky was bluer than the one over Michigan,[21] and twice as big. How about that? I thought. I had frozen to death overnight and somehow qualified for heaven. A run was in order. Maybe a quick five-miler. Out to that boulder and back ought to do it. So off I went. And went, and went, and went. An hour later, the boulder hadn't gotten any bigger or closer. Come to think of it, the 50-foot-tall rock that marked home base behind me hadn't gotten appreciably smaller or more distant in a while, either.

Essence: Are we going to talk about training at some point?

Details: . . .

Stories: No, I think that about covers it.

That about covers it the way cycling shorts about cover things: superficially, but effectively enough. And with plenty of stretch to fit most athletes.

Effort in. Performance out. Results may vary. It's as simple as church and as complicated as school and as arbitrary as either and as good as it gets.

---

19 I'm waiting for science to whip this global-warming thing so it can turn its attention to gravity clusters, but any endurance athlete knows they exist.

20 National Park now, National Monument then.

21 A low bar, to be sure.

THE ECONOMICS

The spending progression goes more or less like this:

Golfers

Triathletes

Bicycle racers

Mountain bike racers

Runners

Swimmers

Ascetic monks

My dad[1]

That's not too flattering. Sure, we're not at the very top of the heap, but being outspent by golfers is a little like smelling nicer than a broccoli fart.

---

1   Whoa. Except for my dad's placement, that's the bad-fashion spectrum, too.

And I'm not even sure we'd cede the top spot to golfers[2] if Rolex watches were lighter and a little more aerodynamic. Golfers blow the mortgage on clubs; we buy bikes. Golfers nick the retirement fund for putters; we do it for carbon race wheels. Golfers arc expensive balls[3] into lakes, woods, and interstate medians[4] several times per round; we suck expensive sugar syrup out of individual foil packets several times per ride. Greens fees, race fees. Country-club memberships, gym memberships. Chest pains, shin splints. Marital counseling . . . marital counseling.

To hell with it. We're not as different from golfers as I'd like to think. Although the two sports couldn't be more different in demand and approach,[5] they are frighteningly close economically, and I don't just mean the numbers. Either sport could be done on the cheap; neither tends to be. Both share the distinction that good equipment truly can improve your results, neither by anywhere near the margin its participants and consumers desperately want to believe.[6]

You play, you pay. Is that a curse? I don't think it is. It's fun to spend money on the right things. It's even motivating. What could be more motivating than getting fast enough to justify that aero helmet you want to buy? This: justifying that aero helmet you just bought.

Economists from Keynes to Friedman[7] say spending money is good, or at the very least inevitable. What you don't want is to spend all that money only to look like a damn fool. You don't want to be the guy going slowly on the expensive bike; you don't want to be the woman whose racing flats gave her shin splints.

You don't want to be the guy who's holding a triathlon book that gives you specific information about equipment that's already out-of-date any more than I want to be the guy who wrote one, if you were wondering where we were[8] headed next. But good judgment and dumb mistakes are timeless, so we've got plenty to cover. Let's get spending.

---

2   Based on a quick survey of *Triathlete* and *Golf Magazine* advertisements.

3   And putters, depending on how the day is going.

4   Not every golf course is Augusta National.

5   I've tried both, and here is what it comes down to: Whenever I've gone golfing, I've looked around the course and thought, "This would be a nice place for a run." I've never been training and thought, "This would be a nice place to whack little balls with sticks."

6   Practitioners of both sports will also insist that theirs is a game of skill, strategy, and conditioning while whipping out the Visa for any new piece of voodoo that claims it will give them an edge.

7   Superfluous information; I'm just dropping names.

8   Which is to say, weren't.

Swim stuff

Swimming looks cheap and still costs a ton.[9] That's because you have to have a place[10] to swim, and there's this thing about getting what you pay for. I don't want to sound elitist, but I have to say a club membership is the way to go. Clubs' pools tend to be available more hours per day. Clubs tend to keep their water at a temperature more suitable for lap swimming. They may attract more serious swimmers, and the more modern ones have separate pools for the less serious swimmers to splash in, throw balls around in, go down slides in, and have certain events in that require everybody to vacate the pool for a day while the staff disinfects the water.

A less expensive option is the pay-per-visit community pool. It's a perfectly good option—water is water—and I used to do all my swimming in the community pool. Now I swim at a YMCA that I like very much. Once a year, the Y closes down for a week, ostensibly for maintenance but in reality, I think, to remind me of just how much I like it there. For a week, I have to plan more carefully because the community pool in the middle school is open for lap swimming only a couple of hours a day. And only for an hour at a time, which turns out not to be as onerous as it seems because the water temperature is set for the Arthritis Aquacise participants, who, it goes without saying, have every bit as much right to the pool as I do. Maybe more, from the look of things. Unrestrained by lane dividers, some of the more relaxed swimmers will float wherever they and their foam noodles and their conversations take them, leaving the lap swimmers to navigate bodies like supply ships navigating through a field of icebergs.[11]

Open water is ostensibly free, but it's seasonal; scarce; dangerous; and, depending on the goose population, unhealthy.[12] But it's really, really cool—and of course, more relevant to triathlon.

Once you've found a place to swim, you've got just a little more spending to do. A suit, yeah, duh. Not much I can tell you that you don't know

---

9   Like certain swimsuits, if you catch my drift.

10   I know. You can swim in a public pool. You can golf on a public course. You can swim in a lake. You can golf in a pasture. I know.

11   There are no absolutes. One of my favorite places to swim is the nearby university's outdoor pool. It's 50 meters long, the water is cool, and the scenery can be stunning. That's a pay-per-use affair, too, until the university goes on a so-called security jag and restricts the pool to tuition-paying students, which suddenly makes the most elite athletic club dues look like pocket change.

12   That's not a typo. I didn't mean to write "shark" or "Portuguese man o' war" or "icky seaweed." A single Canada goose shits a pound a day (so do married ones, but they catch hell if they don't run the fan. But I digress). Jaws may have made the better movie, but coliform bacteria is the scarier predator.

about that. And goggles. I love goggles. I love goggles because they possess the same amount of material and technology as sunglasses at about a fourth to half the price; instead of making me feel stupid for buying sunglasses, this just encourages me to buy more goggles. Which isn't entirely a bad thing because goggles that don't quite fit leak a lot more than sunglasses that don't quite fit. It's also good because there's more to a good fit than the leaking issue. Thomas Hobbes[13] said life could be "solitary, . . . nasty, brutish, and short." That's exactly like a triathlon swim, except it's not solitary or short. You want goggles that will be comfortable to wear a long time and suitable for wearing while being whacked by feet and elbows. Meaning, in my opinion, that those Swedish jobs that fit inside your eye sockets are asking for trouble.[14] Some people like a bigger goggle that's more like a diving mask that leaves your nose free,[15] and with good reason. I like a standard but not excessively low-profile racing goggle. You might or might not. They're cheap enough to experiment with; do so.[16]

Where swim gear gets expensive is the wetsuit. Now. I'm going to tell a joke here that I don't condone or even[17] think funny, but it's a nice metaphor[18] for a lot of equipment:

Q: Why is divorce so expensive?

A: Because it's worth it.

Wetsuits are worth it. You can tell they are because the more elite factions of the open-water-swimming world hate them. Rather, they hate it when other people wear them because wetsuits are an effective equalizer. They keep you warm in cold water when you don't have much body fat. They make you more buoyant when you don't have much body fat. And they float you into a nice position when you don't have much tech-

---

13   Did I really drag a seventeenth-century political philosopher into a discussion of swim goggles? Yes, I did.

14   Too bad, too, because I love them in the pool.

15   Or your great-uncle Virgil's eyeglasses.

16   There are two notable goggle subcategories: prescription lenses and tinted lenses. If you're blind enough, springing for prescription lenses can be a good idea. They're surprisingly inexpensive, probably because they don't have to be as precise as real glasses. Just get your prescription from your eye doctor and order something close. It's not like you're driving in them. That said, I wear contact lenses—90 percent out of vanity. I don't have time in the seconds before the start of the race to look for someone to take my glasses, and I don't feel like spending all that time on dry land, or even the run from the water to the transition area, wearing bug eyes. Tinted lenses are nice, but don't get your hopes up. Triathlons start close to sunup. If the sun is bright, it's going to be bright right at the surface of the water, and nothing short of a welding mask is going to cut the glare. And those fill up with water.

17   Officially.

18   While losing the humor entirely.

nique. It's true: Wetsuits[19] make you swim faster.[20] The worse you swim, the more they help. And when things get vigorous out in the water, you could do worse for body armor. Sorry, purists: Wetsuits rock. They can range widely in price, but they're an advantage at just about any price. More expensive ones and recently made models up and down the range[21] will be much more flexible,[22] buoyant, and slippery. Any wetsuit gives any man a new appreciation for any woman willing to put up with control-top panty hose.

Bike stuff

The bike is where we can spend some real money. How much? As much as you want. How little? Maybe less than you think. All you need, in the purest sense, is a bike that will get you to the finish line safely, and you don't have to race too many times to see some bikes that push even that theory. If you want to finish faster, expensive bikes are nicer than cheap bikes, all things being equal. But all things are seldom equal. Even the inequalities are inconsistent. Once you've got a reasonably light bike that does what it's supposed to, you hit a slope of diminishing returns. But your abilities can affect the slope dramatically. The faster you ride, the more you get out of every dollar spent on aerodynamics. The lighter you are, the more you get out of every dollar spent on reduced weight. That's not very egalitarian, but it is the case.

You want egalitarian? Bike fit is egalitarian. It benefits everyone. Everyone. Whatever you spend on a bike,[23] budget what it takes to buy it from a bike shop that will make sure it fits you.[24] I cannot emphasize this

---

19   We're talking triathlon wetsuits, which are designed for swimming across the surface and then removing quickly, unlike diving wetsuits and surfing wetsuits, which decidedly aren't. The wrong wetsuit will feel claustrophobic, soak up water and scoop up even more, and drag through the water like a barnacle-encrusted garbage scow.

20   There's also a garment called a speed suit, or some such thing. They're for events where the water is too warm to allow wetsuits, and while they have no flotation, they're coated so that they slide through the water like a cooked noodle. They exist so people vastly faster than I can swim slightly faster yet.

21   The technology changes so rapidly, so much, that there's a huge trickle-down effect. This year's flagship is next year's midrange model is two years later's entry-level suit, and they're all good. An old, used wetsuit, conversely, isn't likely to be much of a deal.

22   To the point where I don't see any sense in getting a sleeveless one.

23   Even if you already own a bike.

24   And by this, I do not mean a shop that has you straddle the top tube and feel for a breeze. There's more to fit than getting off the seat without bruising your jewels. It's to the point now that there are franchised bike-fitting systems, which frankly means more to the shops than it means to you. What you want is a shop

enough. Bikes are like shoes. They're complicated. One size, one brand, one pro athlete endorsement does not fit all. There is no best bike. There are so many good bikes that the better plan is to shop for a shop, choose one you like, and then see what bikes it sells. The importance of adopting a shop increases inversely and exponentially in relation to how much you know about fixing bikes.[25] Treat everyone at your shop as though you will someday show up on a Friday afternoon half an hour before they close with a bike that needs a crucial adjustment before Saturday morning's race.[26]

If you get sucked deeply enough into the sport, you'll eventually buy a triathlon-specific bike. Such a bike is more aerodynamic, eases the transition into the run, handles like a puppy on a frozen pond, and instantly alerts packs of roadies to avoid you like a costumed *Star Trek* fan at the Hunting and Fishing Expo. Keep this in mind if you're not yet sure of your level of obsession. You can always buy a road bike and slap aero extensions on the handlebars, then upgrade later to a tri bike. It never hurts to have multiple bikes.[27] Also, procrastination isn't the vice in triathlon that it is in, say, tax preparation or annual physicals. While you get a feel for the sport—and your needs—on your road bike, the new triathlon models will only get better.

Remember that riding naked, though aerodynamic, is otherwise ill-advised, so budget for clothes.[28] And remember you'll spend a lot of time training in them, in a wide variety of conditions. When you try items on, imagine yourself not in the changing room but at mile 98 of a

---

where you feel confident that the staff will spend some time getting one complicated thing (a bike) to fit an even more complicated thing (you). It takes time, and it takes judgment, which takes a certain humility. The shop may charge for these items. That's not soaking you; that's recognizing that the process has value. It often gets folded into the cost of a bike, but whether it does or not, it's worth it.

25   Often, doodly squat. I don't know what it is that makes a bike so mysterious to otherwise smart people, but I've seen college graduates who couldn't get the front wheel off their bike to stow it in the back of the big car they bought to get to their job at the engineering firm.

26   Because you will.

27   Call it a "B" bike, a rain bike, or a backup bike, a second bike can be anything from a luxury to a race-saver—you know, if you make that panicked Friday visit to your bike shop half an hour *after* it closes. Even when everything is going right, sometimes your best bike isn't *the* best bike. One of my favorite races is the Savageman, a half-Iron affair in the Maryland Appalachians that somehow crams 5,900 feet of steep climbing—and thus 5,900 feet of butt-puckering descending—into its 56 bike miles. It was nice to have a bike I didn't steer with my elbows.

28   By which I mean, first and foremost, bike shorts.

truly miserable day. The good stuff is worth the money, and the returns don't diminish.[29]

Spring for bike shoes and the kind of cleat/pedal combination that clicks together like ski bindings. That combination is significantly faster; infinitely more comfortable; and, over time, maybe even cheaper after you spare enough running shoes from the abuse of pedals and toe straps. With a minimum of practice, it doesn't take long to change shoes in the transition zone. Unless you want it to, in which case you've got an excuse to rest while you fumble.

They're going to make you race in a helmet,[30] so buy one that's comfortable, light, and full of vents. The whole point of endurance racing is to get to the point where enough's enough and then keep going. And when enough's enough, the first place you feel it is your head. Baldness is appealing. A shrunken head is appealing. Huge ears that vent heat like a desert jackrabbit's are appealing.[31] The lunch you bought with the money you saved buying the heavier helmet, you don't even remember.

Running stuff

Running shoes are like helmets for your feet, only you don't fall on your head eighty-odd times a minute.

Could anything be worth its price more than your first pair of running shoes? Well, yes: your second pair. And your third pair, and every subsequent pair, which, if you do it right, you'll buy so often you'll feel silly.[32] Keep in mind that you're supposed to throw a helmet away after one impact. It's not asking too much to pitch your shoes after a quarter million or so.

And if I didn't harp on the perils of self-service enough during the bike lecture, it applies tenfold to shoe stores. Buy your running shoes from a running-shoe store. You should look for one with a treadmill because you can take the shoes for test runs while a staff member analyzes your stride. You should look for one where all the salespeople are skinny because that means they're runners, too. You should look for one that sponsors a lot of races because that means it's just cool—and that

---

29   That said, some of the best money you'll spend is on a relatively cheap tube of lube. Tube, stick, jar, whatever. Call it chamois cream, call it blister guard, if it reduces friction in your nether quarters, it's worth whatever it costs, and it doesn't cost much.

30   And besides, you're not a moron.

31   Not really, but if you saw me, you'd understand.

32   Every 300 to 500 miles, depending on whom you ask and how you run. But always long before they look like they need to be replaced.

the owners value the sport and pay attention to it. My[33] running store also hosts clinics, seminars, and even a weekly injury clinic where sports physicians and physical therapists and other people holding impressive degrees will check out problems and answer questions.[34]

Of course, a good running store carries more than shoes. Socks, shorts, tops, jackets, bumper stickers, energy gels and bars—they're all very important, all for countless self-apparent reasons and one subtle

---

33   Note the use of "my." You don't just shop at a good running store; you all but send it Christmas cards and put it in your will.

34   This is like the corner pub hosting a weekly Psychotherapy Night.

one. When you find a good shoe, you should stick with it.[35] This is easier said than done for people with attention spans like mine. You put enough fun, tempting stuff on the clothes side of the store, and I'm less likely to try dumb experiments on the shoe side of the store.[36]

Food stuff

It's cheap. Experiment until race day, and then, for God's sake, whatever you do, don't experiment.

Supplement stuff

A friend of mine was moving from one neighborhood in Los Angeles to another. As the movers were setting down the last of the boxes, one of them sidled up to him and whispered conspiratorially, "We put your stash in the medicine cabinet." Stash? My friend was baffled. He walked to the bathroom, opened the cabinet, and found where the thoughtful mover had discreetly placed the little baggie of catnip.

The point being, it's really hard to keep track of nature's herbs and spices and what's what. Sports supplements are big business. Some of the stuff works, some of it doesn't, some of it is placebo, and some of it's not placebo enough.[37] Don't feel you have to rule it out, but don't be casual. A Los Angeles mover mistook catnip for reefer. That's all I'm saying.

Not material stuff per se

If any one aspect of triathlon is managing to grow faster than triathlon itself, it's professional coaching. It can be one-on-one, hands-on, and expensive as hell, or it can be as cheap as a book. Either can be the best money you spend.[38] Which, duh. Would you buy a Steinway grand and not take piano lessons? On the other hand, either can be a total waste

---

35 Easier said than done when the shoe industry rudely insists on perpetually improving and updating—that is, changing—its products.

36 Don't underestimate the potential disaster here. A couple of years back, I was
deemed experienced enough to take part in a running-shoe testing program at
my store. Experience was crucial because you wanted to be able to see an injury coming when you drew a shoe that didn't turn out to be a good idea for
your build—which happened surprisingly often. That said, don't underestimate
the dangers inherent in riding a particular shoe model into the ground when
there may be better ones out there waiting to be discovered. Thus, don't underestimate the value of a running store with an educated staff and a 30-day, no-
questions-asked return policy.

37 Another friend of mine, a pro cyclist and a damn good one, lost a year of his
career to a suspension from a contaminated supplement. That's not anywhere
near as funny as the catnip story.

38 And I don't need to point out that you've spent a lot.

of money if you choose a coach who's incompatible with you, or if you choose a good one and ignore his or her advice.

The first year I took on a coach, I won my age group for the first time. Also for the second and third time, along with some other nice results that I[39] wasn't used to. I'd like to say that made it worth the money, but it was only a nice bonus. I have never had an injury from triathlon while I've been under his guidance. Not ever. *That* is a bargain.

Check out

Good Lord, you can spend a lot of money in this sport.[40] The good news is, it levels off. You can tell the sport is starting to get a grip on you when you get inordinately excited about going shopping for shiny new triathlon gear. You can tell the sport truly has a grip on you when your stuff is getting a little ragged because you'd rather spend your time using it than shopping for new stuff.

---

39   Not to put too fine a point on it.
40   Why, the other day I had to have all my nice pants taken in at the waist yet again, which isn't technically a triathlon expense, but I'm logging it as one.

CHAPTER 2
Rest Day

GOSH, YOU LOOK GREAT

've always tried to live by the credo, "If you don't know what to do, *do something.*" I learned this from a journalist. When journalists speak candidly about their profession, they're fond of saying, "It's not rocket science."

Christopher Columbus[1] Kraft, Jr. is alleged to have said, "If you don't know what to do, *don't do anything.*" I learned that reading how Kraft was the first person to serve as flight director, and how he built and shaped Mission Control, for NASA.

Hmm.

---

1   Really!

Journalists are also fond of the saying "Consider the source." Better go with the rocket scientist.

Training for triathlons is hard. But, for my money, the hardest part is resting.

And it's the most important part.

I could get all scientific and tell you that the physiological changes you initiate during a long, hard ride don't actually take place until you hit the sack and let your stressed system make the adaptations. I could appeal to hero and celebrity worship and mention that Lance Armstrong[2] claimed that the most common training mistake he saw was people who didn't go hard enough on their hard days and didn't go easy enough on their easy days.[3] I could call up some marginally tangential but oddly relevant analogy like the pause in a monologue, the negative space in a painting, the *autolyse*[4] in bread-baking, or the intermission[5] in an opera.

But I'll go straight for vanity, hedonism, and pride.

Not only is rest a crucial part of making you gorgeous, healthy, and smug; a day off is also a fitting time to reflect on just how gorgeous, healthy, and smug you are.

A couple of days before Ironman Florida, I was a quarter mile off-shore checking out the swim course when I bumped[6] into John. Apologies turned into greetings turned into conversation. John wasn't a boasting kind of guy, so I'm not sure how it came up, but it did:[7] John's racing weight that weekend would be about 165 pounds. John's *deciding-to-race* weight, about a year prior, had been well over 300 pounds.[8] He was, quite literally, half the man he used to be. And from what I could see, he kept the good-looking half.

John—I reiterate, not a boasting kind of guy—acknowledged that I was correct. He wasn't about to make any snide comments about obese people, having spent some time as one himself. With all due respect to two of the best songs ever,[9] Sir Mix-a-Lot's "Baby Got Back"[10] and Queen's "Fat

---

2   Actually, take your pick of sources; this one's an open secret to the point of public domain.

3   Specifically, *because* they didn't go easy enough on their easy days.

4   Bread comes out a whole lot better if you give the dough a 20-minute rest between mixing and kneading it. We could just as easily call it a "rest," but cooking terms just sound *muy bueno* in French.

5   Thank you, Jesus.

6   Quite literally.

7   What, we were supposed to be talking about our stock portfolios out there? That's for golfers.

8   Even the Dow Jones Industrial Average didn't lose that much of itself in a year.

9   Strictly my opinion; I wouldn't think of dragging John into this one.

10   ". . . I like big butts and I cannot lie."

Bottomed Girls,"[11] Louis Prima had it right with "Closer to the Bone."[12] Heavy isn't ugly, and people have their preferences, but physics is physics. Excess weight hides some perfectly good features and makes others sag. It changes posture. It obscures appealing lines and angles. But John was happy to say he liked the way he looked a whole lot better than the way he used to look.

Michelangelo described sculpture as freeing an angel trapped inside marble.[13] John agreed with the emphasis on freedom.[14] The more weight he shed, the easier it became to exercise and shed more weight yet. The less skin he had, the more comfortable he was in less clothing, so the more sun he got and the better his complexion became. But the big difference, he said, is that he just smiles more these days.

John's story is impressive but hardly isolated. He's not even the only halfperson I've met. He's certainly not the only triathlete to drop a few pounds; in fact, it's tough to find a triathlete who hasn't. In a culture that's obsessed with losing weight, it's worth noting that in sports like triathlon it just sort of happens.[15]

Not that every triathlete shares, or eventually shares, or even should share, a body type with a hungry heron. This sport gives as well as it takes, and at the very least, it rearranges what's there. Muscle gets a little more defined. Posture gets a little more upright. There's a growing, almost disconcerting new affinity toward the kind of formfitting clothing that's appropriate to the sport.[16]

There is also, I don't know, let's call it grace: a certain appeal that goes with some sort of a spring in your step. Have you ever noticed that some movie actors look fine in still photos but ooh-la-la in motion?[17] Triathlons not only foster strong, lean legs, but imbue an efficiency of stride that translates into . . . yes, let's go ahead and call it grace.

"Geez, Jef," you're thinking, "at this point, why don't we just call it narcissism?" And you have a point. It's getting a little thick in here. Fear

---

11   ". . . You make the rockin' world go 'round."
12   ". . . Sweeter is the meat."
13   "Carving is easy; you just go down to the skin and stop."
14   Didn't seem as impressed with the whole Michelangelo name-dropping effort.
15   When I went to race Ironman Florida, my flights in and out of Panama City's tiny airport were on a plane filled with triathletes. It was startling. Lord, did the airlines save some money on fuel that week.
16   Critics of the skintight garment are hereby invited to look up old photos from the era of, say, Paavo Nurmi and tell me the pantaloons on those guys are anything to return to.
17   This is not universal. Rodney Dangerfield always had a spring in his step, but it never conveyed much more than the impression of a man who'd been locked out of the bathroom.

not. This is just a little rest-day audit of benefits. Even Bill Gates balances his checkbook so he can enjoy seeing that he's in the black.[18] And if we're still smug and self-satisfied and full of ourselves, well, that's why we have race photographers.

Nobody—*nobody*—makes it more than a race or two before the rose in the mirror wilts under the cold eye of a digital camera. What feels to the soul like life turned up to 10 shows up on the computer screen resembling a string of zeroes, where 10 equals petting a purring kitten and 1 equals giving it a pill and a bath; where 10 is Andy Hampsten climbing the Gavia Pass on his way to winning the 1988 Giro d'Italia and 1 equals, well, me looking completely thrashed after last Saturday's Run for the Ronald McDonald House—after running just 5 km; cooling down; trotting back to join my wife, who was walking the course; and accompanying her to the finish line so the photographer could take her picture while I still looked like I was being administered a spinal tap with a whittled stick.[19]

And that's why it's OK to spend a little bit of your rest day back in front of the mirror, pointing and winking and making that little *tchk-tchk* sound. You've earned it, you need it, or both. Enjoy it. You gorgeous hunk o' humanity, you.

---

18 At least, I bet he does. You know what else I bet? I bet he does it right there in the check register, with a pen, because *he can*.
19 Meaning it is, for me, a typical running photo.

GOSH, YOU FEEL GREAT

I t was at a Dizzy Gillespie concert that I tried alcohol[1] for the first time. Dizzy seemed to approve; he paused between numbers to say, to no one in particular,[2] for no reason in particular:[3]

> **"If it's good *to* ya, it's gotta be good *fo'* ya."**

It made sense to me. I poured myself another plastic cup of white wine,[4] and then another, and that might have been it, or it might not—and Dizzy played on. The evening was good to me, and it looked like it was good to Dizzy.

In retrospect, Dizzy may have been a higher authority on what was good *to* me than what was good *fo'* me. The next morning, my first hangover seemed good neither to nor fo'.

---

1   A bit bland for bebop, but fully in the spirit of it for a choirboy from the country.
2   Though I took him to mean me.
3   Though I took him to mean with regard to my vague pangs of guilt (see "choirboy," note 1).
4   You were expecting Jägermeister? Again, please see "choirboy," note 1.

I'm feeling fine now, thank you. I don't breathe hard unless I want to. I don't feel my muscles burn unless I want to. I don't feel my heart pound unless I want to. I don't run out of gas unless I want to. The thing is, I *do* want to because the racing pulse and the shortness of breath and the pain and the weakness are all part of the process that gives me wings. Life is good.[5] Dizzy didn't have it wrong; he just got the order mixed up. If I may revise:

"If it's good *fo'* ya, it's gotta be good *to* ya."

This is not graduate-level stuff. Remember John from the previous section? The one who lost half his weight? Right. That John. Forget John. He's so successful he's almost abstract. Meet Al.

My friend Al finally bought a nice bike. Al did already own a bike, an ancient Schwinn that could anchor an aircraft carrier. I mention this for the benefit of an endless parade, past and future, of (occasionally but by no means universally) well-meaning, budget-conscious monks and cheapskates who question, scold, or excoriate me for advocating the purchase of what seems to them to be a needlessly expensive bicycle. The pattern is predictable. Only the level of vitriol changes.

"That's a lot of money," the lecture begins. "A bike is a bike." Then, "I've got [or, once in a while, "can get cheap"] a perfectly good bike." The crescendo starts to build into a rant. "I'm not a serious cyclist, so a serious bike is a waste," or "I'll try riding a cheap bike and see if I like it." But then a wrong turn into "I don't really need to go fast anyway" hints at a basic understanding and acknowledgment of my point, which doesn't sit well and thus prompts varying levels of assault on my elitist, snobbish character, inspiring newfound self-confidence in the plaintiff's self-appointed expertise and bringing on the inevitable flash of insight and coup de grace: "I'll get more exercise if I ride a worse bike!"

Here's the thing about Al's "perfectly good" Schwinn: *He never, ever wanted to ride it.* The new bike weighed about 20 pounds. Al weighed 170 pounds. Three weeks later,[6] Al and the bike *together* weighed 170 pounds. Al loves riding this bike everywhere. He really loves no longer having to carry the equivalent *of* his new bike everywhere he goes. The bike is good *for* him. The bike is good *to* him.

There's more to it than weight. An active body is simply a nicer place to live. Sleep comes easy, swift, and deep. Appetites more closely mirror needs. The occasional binge is less consequential. Stronger muscles

---

5   And all four of my cheeks are smaller than all four of Dizzy's cheeks were, for what that's worth.

6   !

support the frame with less pain, fatigue, and risk. Everything is easier. Systems simply work better.[7]

---

7   "Better" doesn't necessarily mean "perfectly." I have cholesterol issues. My LDL, or "bad" cholesterol level, is normal, but my level of HDL, or "good" cholesterol, gooses the number to the high side. The good ratio doesn't give me a free pass around the high total, my doctor tells me, but neither does she seem too worried. She doesn't even see a need to change my diet, though she did once tell me studies showed cholesterol could respond well to something called psyllium. She didn't mention that psyllium was the main ingredient in stuff like Metamucil, though the pharmacist explained it nicely, if a little more loudly than I considered absolutely necessary. The embarrassment was easy enough to brush off, considering that (a) my audience mostly comprised people waiting for pills to treat conditions no less embarrassing than the one suggested by my brand-new tub of laxative; and (b) clearly, exercise has been proven to enhance mental health as much as physical health.

Including the system of neurons, axons, dendrites, and fear of boats[8] that form the mental aspect of one's being. I'm not a neurologist or a psychologist or a psychiatrist or even especially good at noticing when I'm getting on people's nerves, but I've got enough experience with both sides of the whole *mens sana in corpore sano*[9] thing to know it works. I'm smarter when I'm fitter, or at least smart enough to believe it's so and behave accordingly. I'm also happier when I'm fitter. Some of that is chemical,[10] sure, but some of it is because it's simply fun out there. Henry David Thoreau said, "Life sucks; get out of the house." Maybe not quite in those words,[11] but that's the gist, and I have to agree. You can't run away from your problems, but it can't hurt to make them chase you once in a while.

A writer I know[12] said everybody should play a team sport because teammates never put up with your crap. They don't want to hear excuses, they won't wait for you if you're late, and they don't care where your picture is on the org chart at your boring-ass corporation. They expect you to show up, shut up,[13] put up, and play. Although triathlon is an individual sport on the surface, most triathletes find other athletes to train with, and should.[14] The same social reality checks apply, and they're more refreshing than you'll believe.

Everything I've mentioned so far is beginner-to-novice stuff, where the gasping and palpitations and pain of a hard race or workout are a means to an end, a small price to pay to get healthy and feel good.

---

8   This may just be me.

9   "A healthy mind in a healthy body," but it sounds better the way the Roman poet Juvenal wrote it. The brand name "Asics" is an acronym for *anima sana in corpore sano*—same diff but with a more kinetic vibe to it, not to mention it's easier than going to a store and asking for a shoe called "Msics."

10 Cue up another bebop lifestyle reference, but work beta-endorphins into it somewhere.

11 In *these* words: "The mass of men lead lives of quiet desperation" and "An early morning walk is a blessing for the whole day."

12 Okay, I'll drop the name: Randy Wayne White, whose columns in *Outside* magazine 20 years ago were good enough to convince me I'd never be able to write that well and wonderful enough that I had to try.

13 I confess I have trouble with this one.

14 The options are plentiful. Many cities have triathlon clubs, and they welcome new members with genuinely open arms. If there is no club, triathletes are everywhere, typically friendly, and happy to associate with other people who get it. And remember, as a multisport athlete, you've got three times the options if you want to train with the, ah, less diverse. Runners and swimmers love triathletes because we're typically not specialized enough to beat them, but we're stubborn enough to keep up. Cyclists aren't as open at first, but that's more of a safety thing. Once you prove you can hold a straight line and not cause crashes, and especially if you leave the twitchy tri bike at home and ride a road bike, they'll usually let you join. Which doesn't mean they'll put up with your crap.

Eventually you'll get to a point where those sensations themselves feel good. Seriously. That searing feeling in your lungs might as well be the whine of a sports car's engine at redline. That's how it is for me, anyway. I'd like to think it's because I'm just so goshdarn tough, but it's really just that I've finally figured out that the pain is self-inflicted and temporary. It's easy to tolerate a certain amount of discomfort when you know the pain goes away the instant you back off the throttle.

And when you back off the throttle in a greater sense, it feels even better. I know it sounds like hitting yourself on the head with a flyswatter because it feels so good when you stop,[15] but there's more to it than that. Training is essentially a calculated process of tearing down your body while it rebuilds itself into something stronger. But there's a delay factor built in that lasts as long as a week or two. If you take a break from tearing down your body, it doesn't stop building itself up for a while. You throw off the equilibrium. You're a fighter jet on the flight deck, engines winding up with wheels locked in place, an expanding fireball of potential energy and testosterone.[16] If you do it before a big race, it's called tapering. If you do it just because, or if it is forced on you by outside circumstances, it may be less focused, but it's no less effective.

Work hard, and you can take on the day. Rest up, and you feel like you can take on the world. Oh, my, but that feels good.

And if it's good *to* ya . . . or is it, if it's good *fo'* ya . . . ?

Whatever. I ran hard, and I'm too buzzed to care.

---

15   I believe the actual cliché is hitting yourself on the head with a hammer, but that's just stupid.

16   Just an expression, ladies.

GOSH, YOU'RE CRANKY, IRRITABLE, AND IMPOSSIBLE TO LIVE WITH

Too much of a good thing is wonderful.

Mae West generally gets credit for the quip, but so many people over so many years[1] have used the phrase so many times that it has sunk into useless cliché. Which teaches us two lessons. One, if you want the lion's share of the credit for what's a more or less established, universal quotation, it doesn't hurt to make it vaguely naughty and have a

---

1 All the way back to Shakespeare, in *As You Like It*: "Why then, can one desire too much of a good thing?" which really gets you thinking. What could possibly constitute too much of a good thing in sixteenth-century England? *Two* bowls of gruel? A whole week without plague? Those insufferable Puritans finally leaving the neighborhood on ye horse ye rode in on?

memorable set of knockers.[2] Two, not only can you get too much of a good thing; apparently you can get too much of Too Much of a Good Thing.

So we're going to have to admit that there's such a thing as too much triathlon, too. And by too much triathlon, I mean too much training and I mean too much rest.

Big surprise, huh? Isn't excess sort of the point of triathlon or any other endurance sport?

Big surprise: I'm going to come out and say it is not. The point of triathlon is to find the line where enough is enough and one step farther is too much; to tease Cerberus, the three-headed[3] hound at the gates of Hades, without getting bit. Stepping over the line is not a trespass to be punished; it's information that comes at a price. It is not the point of it all.

Besides, excess is a moving target. Cerberus is not some lethargic, sedentary bloodhound; he's a nervous, hyperkinetic little dachshund,[4] bouncing off the walls and skittering underfoot, and sometimes the only way to know where he's standing is to cross him.

It's easy to cross the line without knowing it. Somebody has to say it: We triathletes are tough. We've got a high pain tolerance, and we're fit. Things that make other people suffer don't make us suffer so much. Also, we're goal-oriented and can be vulnerable to bouts of tunnel vision.[5] So we cross the line unawares and recognize our transgression in retrospect. *What's that pain in my heel? Why am I walking funny? Is it tendinitis? Is it a pulled muscle? A stress fracture?* It is Cerberus, growling through his teeth, flopping around down there, up to his gums in gastrocnemius.

That's how we find out we've overdone it with the training, anyway. It's very cut-and-dried and bruised and mauled. Overdoing the rest and recovery is a little more subtle and insidious and must be pointed out to us by those we love because we are driving them *straight up the frigging wall.*

Too much rest can manifest itself in a short temper, a whiny voice, unpredictable moods, an irrepressible need to fidget, and a strange merger of the panicked suspicion that in just a few days you've managed to lose 12 months' worth of conditioning while achieving the subcutaneous profile of a sea lion with an insatiable desire for the kind of food they put in the aisles toward the middle of the supermarket where small children are throwing

---

2   Since this will come up sooner or later, H. L. Mencken had man-boobs.

3   I keep telling you, three is the magic number.

4   Or at least that's how I enjoy picturing him. I also like to envision the god Hades following along with the leash in one hand, a baggie and a sippy cup full of coffee in the other, wearing Bermuda shorts pulled up too far, sandals, black calf-highs, and an "I'd rather be fishing" gimme hat and still somehow thinking it's the three-headed wiener dog that has all the neighbors looking at him funny.

5   In the sense that dung beetles can be vulnerable to bad breath.

tantrums. In fact, too much rest would be completely indistinguishable from some kind of unisex premenstrual syndrome but for the lack of a deep compulsion to go cruising the clearance racks at the shoe store.[6]

I[7] can start showing symptoms after as few as two consecutive days of idleness. Within three or four days, I enter an illogical but undeniable mode in which whatever extra hours I've gained from not training have simply disappeared, if the amount of stuff I'm getting accomplished is any indication. Anything beyond that and I'm a candidate either for therapy or a leading role in a Kafka novel.

I don't know exactly what causes it, if it's a weakness in the triathlete personality or an addict's symptoms of withdrawal from some cocktail of beta-dopa-endorphinated self-generated chemicals, or if we just work ourselves into such a superior physical and mental state that it's a disappointment to come down from Olympus and live once again with the mortals,[8] but it's horrible.

It's simply horrible. And if it didn't happen like that, I would have to figure out a way to work it so it did. Honestly, it almost feels like I'm running a scam: I screw up or catch a spell of bad luck and get hurt or fall behind on work or other obligations. Something has to go for a while, and this time it's training.[9] It works, a little, for a while, but after a couple of days, the black bile builds and I start behaving like the cartoon guy on the "Give Me My Coffee and Nobody Gets Hurt" mug. The most immediately obvious solution to the problem seems to be to work harder and longer, train less, and spiral into a deeper and darker antisocial, depressive funk. But no! The very people who need my love, my effort, my sparkling personality, and my time suggest—nay, prescribe or even demand—that I drop those very obligations and responsibilities and go immediately for a ride, run, or swim, or even a walk.[10] Leave the heart rate monitor or

---

6   This thesis is open to, and perhaps destined for, debate, so let me state my rebuttal in advance: You're right, you're absolutely right, I don't know what I was thinking, and I love you very, very much.

7   According to reliable sources.

8   Yeah, right, I bet that's the one.

9   This choice can actually sound reasonable in the moment. Training takes a lot of time, and the whole idea, unless you are a pro (which, right), is that training and racing relieve stress rather than exacerbating it.

10   Or an aquajog, a stationary, seemingly pointless run with a flotation belt around your waist in the deep end of the pool. I haven't forgotten that these layoffs can be due to injury as well as to being a responsible grown-up. The effectiveness of aquajogging, and the ability to do it while recovering from just about any injury short of gangrene, is equaled only by its tedium. But if you can handle the monotony, there is no better workout or therapy when you're injured or recovering from a hard effort. (NB: A quick Internet search fails to confirm whether "aquajog"

power meter at home; even a quick[11] 5-mile run if that's all I can swing. Just get out and train.

And it works! I come home from what feels like an unforgivable indulgence, and instantly, noticeably, profoundly, one or two of us[12] are feeling one or two worlds' less weight on our shoulders. It's the damnedest thing.

Wait. No. *This* is the damnedest thing: You can see it coming every single time, slowly, surely, and from a long way off, as ominous and inevitable as the tall-masted battleship HMS *Despondence* bearing down on you across the open sea in a musty breeze. That's life sometimes, and by now you know to accept it. All you can do is offer apologies in advance, have your thanks ready for the future, and have your chain lubed or your shoes powdered so you're ready to fly even before they finish saying, "Oh, for God's sake, just *go*."

What have we learned from all this?

1. Yes, there can be too much of a good thing.
2. But it's neither wonderful nor horrible, virtue nor vice, just information.
3. Too much rest is a peculiarly insidious form of excess.
4. Once you've crossed the line, you simply need to cross back.
5. Which isn't as simple as it seems.
6. But a surprisingly large population is eager to help you.
7. Meaning a larger population than you thought Gets It.
8. Though they don't pick up on these subtleties immediately, another reason to think of triathlon as a lifetime sport.
9. If you're looking for a triathlon—or life—mission statement, you could do much worse than "Oh, for God's sake, just *go*."

---

is a registered trademark before I'm fatally distracted by the news that *there is an aquajogging world championship.* I don't think I can ever trust the Internet again.)

11   Another bonus of this beautiful sport: Your spouse can suggest a "quickie," and it can have double the meaning, both equally wonderful.

12   And maybe this is why it works. Much as the advice benefits the mopey, oxygen-deprived athlete, it has got to be a pleasure to have our grouchy asses out from underfoot. In fact, if triathlon gear manufacturers advertised on television (which they don't, and I think that says something profound all by itself), here's their commercial, with my compliments: Camera shows a triathlete who is "off his feed," as we farm boys say. Wife convinces grouch to lighten up and go ride for an hour. As soon as he's out the garage door, there's a knock at the front door. It's the massage therapist, chocolate in one hand, a Jennifer Weiner novel in the other, and a look that says she's never even heard of a brick or a kilojoule, let alone been inclined to squeeze them into every possible conversation. Fade to black with the tagline "Tri-Supply Sports. Yeah, sure it's for him." You're welcome. Obviously, the gender roles can be switched, but then take care to switch out the Jennifer Weiner or you'll ruin the whole thing.

CHAPTER 3

The Race

THE RACE PREPARATION

I remember being young and foolish[1] and convinced quite to my satisfaction that it made sense to take out a bank loan to buy a toy, in this case a hang glider.[2] My father,[3] to my surprise, agreed and told me about a revolutionary new program at the local savings and loan, a kind of reverse loan where I would identify what I wanted to buy and then, before I bought it, establish a term, break it down into monthly installments, and begin making payments. And get this: Instead of making me pay interest on the loan, the bank would actually pay *me* since I was duping it into holding on to my money before I spent it. After the payments were made, I'd go buy my hang glider, and everybody would be happy. I don't know how my dad kept a straight face, but he did while I swallowed

---

1 Let me count the ways, in the remainder of this sentence alone.
2 At least it wasn't a motorcycle.
3 Who prefers to call himself "cheap" instead of "economical" because it uses less typewriter ribbon.

the whole thing like a fruity-sweet Flintstones vitamin. It wasn't until he actually came clean and used the words "savings account" that he broke character and snorted. Hard. I remember hoping it hurt a little.

I saved my money, bought my hang glider, and forgave my dad, perhaps in that order but not necessarily. The glider was fun for about five years, and I've been without serious money problems ever since.[4] With one exception.[5] Meanwhile, I've heard friends complain about the payments on their excessively nice cars and houses and toys and wish there were a system in place where you did the hard part first and ultimately got to enjoy the fruits of your labors without strings attached.

I'd send those people to my dad, but I think his straight-face talents peaked on that day in 1978. Besides, I guess I've been saving his reverse-loan scam[6] for this very section.

It's race week now. You've done the hard part. You've made the payments, so to speak. The hang glider, the expensive car, whatever metaphor, it's yours now. You've tinkered with the engine,[7] bored the cylinders, filled it with premium, and polished the fenders. Time to slam the hood, pull the keys out of your pocket, and say, "All right. Let's see what this baby can do."

Here's what this baby does, what I do, when I've got a race coming up: I get really, really nervous. Let me repeat that for emphasis: I've been racing triathlons, and the elements that make up triathlon, for essentially my entire adult life. And still, before any race, every race, from a priority-A pressure cooker to a kinda-sorta meaningless[8] race for the hell of it, I am as nervous as a testicle at a Polar Plunge.[9]

Psychologists tell me this[10] comes from DNA still hanging around from an era when my ancestors lived on the open savannah and wore animal skins and thought five cogs were plenty enough gears for anybody and hunted with sharp sticks in a world where you killed your dinner or your dinner killed you, when butterflies in your gut and ice in your veins enabled you to fight or flee and live another day and pass those brave genes along to progeny that eventually would hunt not with sharp sticks on the savannah but with currency and credit cards at the drive-up

---

4   Thanks, Dad.
5   Until I discovered real airplanes; even if you're not a car person, motors are nothing but trouble.
6   Ibid.
7   I guess it's the car.
8   Well, there's one problem right there; they all mean the world to me.
9   Half the population can just trust me on this one, and I'm not implying half the population has done a Polar Plunge.
10   My nerves, not my questionable taste in simile and metaphor.

window of Deep-Fry Delight and still be killed by its dinner, just a little more slowly.[11]

What I'm getting at is that the bubbling going on in your gut has valid origins, and if it hasn't gone away in two million years of human evolution, it's not going away before the weekend. I certainly haven't vanquished it in my own 20-odd years of racing things, and I'm not sure I want to. In fact, I'm sure I don't want to.

The butterflies are my friends now, and they are everything I could want in a friend.[12] They give me pep talks; they keep me honest; they tip me off when something big is about to happen. They are rock-solid reliable, and as surely as I can count on them to show up, I can count on them to leave on time.[13]

But you know how some of your friends are low-maintenance[14] and some are high-maintenance[15] and some are a restraining order waiting to happen?[16] Right. You don't want your friend the butterflies getting out of control. So after all that training, you're not done preparing. You'll want to spend the days before the race wiping out a few final worries to ensure that your nerves enhance the experience instead of dominating it.

Like, back off the training. In an era when you can order something from across the country and see the merchandise on your doorstep the next morning, training is maddeningly retro. You cannot FedEx fitness. Did you have a nice, hard workout? Good for you. Please allow 10 to 14 days for shipping, handling, and physiological adaptation. Meanwhile, the bill arrives immediately. Put another way, if you flog yourself silly the week before you race, you can look forward to reaping the benefits the week after the race is over while feeling knackered and worthless right away.

This is not a call to buy a recliner and a one-week subscription to the Three Stooges channel. You don't want to completely forget what forward motion feels like. Work on your form, fine-tune your transitions,[17] maybe

---

11 Genes involving focus and staying on task were not handed down so efficiently, apparently. Not to my corner of the species, anyway.

12 And more, I'm afraid. Visits to my real friends don't generally have me standing in the long line outside the Port-O-Lets.

13 Specifically, when the gun goes off or the horn sounds or whatever they do to start the race. The nerves build and build and build, and then, *powie!* The stress is gone in an instant. Pre-race nerves are like sermons, drum solos, and railroad crossings: They're a lot easier to enjoy if you know when they're going to end.

14 "Has it really been 20 whole years?"

15 "I know, I'm sorry, it's been two whole days."

16 "I *did* check caller ID! He called from a cell phone!"

17 Yes, your neighbors will wonder as they watch you practice changing shoes on the fly. So what? They've been wondering about you ever since they first saw you roll out of the driveway in bike shorts and a sleeveless top.

enjoy a short burst of speed here and there. Do what you want; just don't get tired doing it. How cool an assignment is that?

So you'll have a little time on your hands. Use that time, and some of your nervous energy, to get your stuff together. And that's not a politely watered-down, otherwise vaguely crude idiom. I really do mean "stuff." Grab a checklist, lay out all your gear, and pack it up in your duffel bag or backpack or whatever you're using. Do this a day or two in advance for three primary reasons: First, it's nice to be able to take your time. Second, it takes more time than you think, and too much confidence will make you late for the race or late for bed the night before the race, or both, and intolerably grumpy in any event. Finally, and most importantly for obsessive-compulsive types,[18] it gives you the chance to panic and repeatedly check your bag in the comfort of your home instead of on the way to the race. Which is no guarantee, sadly, that you won't spend the drive to the race weaving down the road with one hand on the wheel and the other digging around in your bag.[19] But like chicken soup and fresh undies, it can't hurt.[20]

Speaking of chicken soup,[21] nutrition is often the last pre-race frontier. What do you put in your stomach to keep the butterflies company?

Good news or bad, this is one of those situations where you can't work any last-minute miracles, but you can choose from a buffet[22] of last-minute disasters. Obviously,[23] the night before your race is not the time to try the discount sushi or the rare, rare, rare ribeye or the nearly recognizable leftovers cowering in the hindmost regions of the refrigerator like so many nerds in a gym-class dodgeball game.

---

18 Me. You. Everyone.

19 Grief-saving tip for neurotics: Put your helmet, your shoes, and your goggles on top of the bag's contents. If you've got those, you can forget just about anything else and get away with it.

20 Not that it will necessarily help. I throw this advice around as if I've got it all under control, but in truth I'm the athletic embodiment of the nut who worries his vacation away wondering if he left the iron turned on. How bad is it? Unless I'm flying to a race, or carpooling with several friends and limited space, I will pack a *whole separate bag* with duplicates of everything in the first bag. Just in case everything in my triathlon gear gets switched with, I don't know, picnic supplies. Even though I have never once had to pull anything from the duplicate bag. This doesn't heavily endorse my claims that this sport is good for my mental health, does it?

21 Okay. Somebody needs to work on his transitions, and I don't mean changing shoes.

22 All too literally: How much gear, training, and vacation time are you willing to bet on the efficacy of that pane of glass suspended between somebody's sneeze and your whipped potatoes?

23 Or not so obviously: Stories of food-poisoning meltdowns among the pros—professionals!—are not unheard-of.

But there's no point in overcompensating. By overcompensating, I mean things like carbohydrate loading. You'll still hear "Born to Be Wild" on the PA by the finish line, so I shouldn't be surprised that people are forever asking about a dietary trend from the same era. And just as "Born to Be Wild" is still a perfectly good song, carbo-loading is still a valid way of boosting fuel stores for longer events. But both are a wee bit long in the tooth, and I daresay the song holds up better. Also, amateurs tend to get it wrong. For every Karaoke John Kay singing "Kick the world in a lovin' place," there are a hundred people[24] who think carbo-loading is the all-you-can-eat pasta special at Vermicelli's.[25] I'm no dietician,[26] but from what I've read, studied, and tried, nutrition works the same way as anything else: Consistency beats the quick fix every time. As Billy Joel[27] would sing, halfway between Steppenwolf and Bon Jovi and halfway between carbo-loading and Power Bars, "Don't go changing."

My dad had it right: Plan, save, and enjoy the payoff unencumbered by debt. Good advice. And I still found a way to get into money trouble while following it. Hang gliding led to flying airplanes, and I followed his advice for that, too. I saved my money in advance, and when I had enough for ground school and lessons, I cashed out and got my pilot's license. What I hadn't absorbed was the fact that sometimes when you save and prepare and do everything right and then buy the dream, you're only beginning to spend.

Tomorrow is race day. You've trained. You've geared up. You've prepared. You've made the deposits, collected the interest. Today you'll cash out your account, ready to race, free and clear. This time tomorrow, you'll already be overdrawn, doomed to a lifetime of running—and swimming and cycling—to catch up.

And that's one deficit-based microeconomy even my dad can get behind.

---

24   Yet another entirely made-up statistic.

25   It's not. It's a complicated and undignified process of depleting your reserves in order to make your body crave carbohydrates and thus be open to absorbing more than the normal quota, followed by capitalizing on that openness; that is, making a pig of yourself. Lovely. By the time Steppenwolf was giving way to Bon Jovi (all right, *you* try and find a decent rousing anthem from the 1980s), distance runners were figuring out what bicycle racers had known all along: Just eat something during the race.

26   Like that's stopped anybody else from offering an opinion; advice; or, all too often, a product.

27   No rousing anthems here, either!

THE RACE

O h, hey. It's race day, and I see you've got time to do a little reading before you get wet. Either you've got an evening triathlon[1] or you are, like me, an early riser. I like to get up a minimum of four hours before the start of the race. There are a lot of good reasons to do it that way.[2] It's a good nutrition strategy to get some food into yourself with time to turn[3] it into usable fuel instead of gastric bilge.[4] It's a good organizational approach,[5] allowing a little more time to check and double-check gear and route and schedule without rushing. It's nice to see the sun rise. But really, it's much simpler than all that. These races are hard enough as it is. I can't imagine doing one while I'm still trying to wake up.

If the race is far enough away or big enough that I need a hotel room, I can usually sign in and pick up my numbers the night before the race.[6] Otherwise, I like to get to the venue as soon as they'll let me in. The lines are shorter at registration; at body numbering; and, let's face it, at the

---

1   Rare as a Marlboro ad in *Running Times*.
2   None of which *my* wife buys into, either.
3   Most of.
4   And the rest into, ah, jetsam, as long as we're co-opting nautical terms.
5   I know. Me. But blind sows and acorns and all that.
6   Or if it's in the town where I live, but in that case I'm probably also helping out.

loo.[7] The promoters and volunteers are less rushed, more able to help when I ask things like how small I can cut and tape down my bike number.[8] If transition-zone spots are first come, first served, I've got a better choice. Same with parking spaces.[9] And after I fumble around setting up my stuff in the dark,[10] I can spend an hour and a half getting bored and cold. It's a good plan. It is not a perfect plan.

Half an hour or so before the race starts, I'll start getting warmed up. My cerebrum has always bought into the importance of a good warm-up, but I'll confess my brain stem still wonders sometimes. In a pursuit that burns this much energy, it seems odd to squander so many kilojoules[11] when the clock isn't even running and you're going to have to stand around waiting for instructions and national anthems and schedule glitches anyway. But[12] the brain stem alone is not to be trusted. It truly is good to warm up. The shorter the event, the longer the warm-up, but always, at a minimum, work yourself into that first chill of a breaking sweat. There are myriad physiological explanations for how this benefits us, but I do better picturing it this way: Sooner or later, like about ten feet from shore, I'll have to make an uncomfortable surge. And my body can either go *"What the . . . ?"* or go, *"Oh, this again."*

In the moments before the race begins, I'm a Saint Elmo's fireball of escalating stress, fear, and uncertainty; then somebody issues a command and there is a burst of intense discomfort and everything is different. The temperature changes, I don't weigh anything, sounds are muffled, there's an odd feeling of peace amid the fury, and I wonder if this is what it's like to die. And if it is, then it doesn't sound too bad if when I die, the next thing I do is go for a bike ride.[13]

At some point I'll feel like I'm running out of air, and it's once again time for my cerebrum to remind my brain stem to shut the hell up and quit panicking. What feels like a shortage of oxygen is actually a sensation triggered by a surplus of carbon dioxide, and it's easily rectified by

---

7　That's United Kingdom–ish for "pissoir."

8　I'm convinced that the real aerodynamic advantage to those flat, wide down-tubes is the way you can use clear electrical tape to adhere your number flush with the surface.

9　This one my wife can get behind.

10　Twenty of the best dollars you'll ever spend on tri equipment is one of those goofy little LED headlamps.

11　I was surprised to hear my brain stem use a big word like "kilojoules," too.

12　If we've learned anything from slot-machine players, disgraced televangelists, and whoever thought it might be a good idea to make Howard the Duck into a movie (or anyone who thought *Howard the Duck* might be a good movie for a first date, for that matter, although Patty and I are still married),

13　Major religions have been founded on shakier premises.

relaxing a moment and remembering to exhale all the way. The brain stem gets this all wrong and tells me to do the opposite, to hoard some extra air in my lungs and to kick harder and windmill my arms in order to get as quickly as possible to the next opportunity for a breath, which, at that rate, I need ever and ever sooner. My brain stem is a moron. It's no wonder it gets stuffed way in the back, where it has to listen to the temporal lobe go on and on about the good old days.

I still have to remind myself to watch where I'm swimming. It's not that lifting my eyes out of the water and sighting on a landmark is that difficult or slows me down that much. I just forget. Swimming is all about body position and rhythm, and lifting my eyes just above the surface of the water feels like it's messing up both, and, you know, what's the harm in trusting my inner compass for a few more strokes at a time? The harm is that a few strokes at a time, a few degrees off at a time, add up, and in too many races I have finally lifted my head to take a bearing and noticed that I was alone, either leading the race or off on my own private cruise. And I'm not the kind of swimmer who ever leads the race.

As I come in toward shore, my brain stem and cerebrum are having another go at it. My BS sees that it's shallow enough to stand up and suggests we do so. My C knows how much effort it is to wade with any speed and that I'm going to need those legs for the rest of the race. C knows my best bet is to leap and dive, leap and dive, swooping like a dolphin up to the shallows. And a compromise is reached in my head, with BS agreeing to continue swimming past the waders whose cerebrums lost that argument until my fingers all but brush the sand, whereupon C agrees to have me wade in rather than dolphin-leap because it looks great when the elites do it but pretentious when guys like me do it.

Every single race, I marvel at how far the transition zone is from the water.[14] It's no biggie. It's actually nice, as it gives me time to peel off the top half of my wetsuit[15] and then pull off my goggles and swim cap,[16] and it knocks some of the sand off my feet before I stuff them into my bike shoes.

First thing I do in transition after I peel my wetsuit the rest of the way off is put on my helmet and buckle it. This keeps me from getting disqualified for something as stupid as getting on my bike without a buckled

---

14 I don't know why I marvel at this. If it were my park, I wouldn't put the parking lot right next to the water, and I wouldn't want the race director to let hundreds of triathletes push their bikes across my grass.

15 Do that first.

16 Do that second. That way you're not trying to undress with a handful of plastic and silicone.

helmet. Besides, my head is as good a place as any to keep my helmet[17] while I mess with the rest of my transition, which essentially consists of grabbing my bike and pushing it out to where I can get on it and start riding. I have triathlon-specific bike shoes that I leave clipped into my pedals, not because it's any easier to put my shoes on that way but because it allows me to do it once I'm on the bike and enjoying motion, any motion, toward the finish line.[18]

Out on the road, on my bike, I'm in my element. That's not as good as it sounds. It puts me in the most danger of screwing up and either getting busted for drafting as I pick my way through the crowd or getting a little too happy and squandering caloric currency that I'm really going to miss during the last two miles of the run. I could blame myself, and should, but it's more rewarding to blame the slower cyclists who started before me or swam that much faster. It's fun passing people, enough fun to foster delusions of competence. It's no fun getting passed on the run by those same people while you're stumbling cross-eyed through your own personal purgatory, and I don't think it's asking too much for them to shoulder some of the responsibility. Okay, maybe it is. Until you factor in drafting worries. Not only is it fun to pass other cyclists; you're supposed to do it quickly so you don't benefit from the reduced wind resistance in their slipstream.[19] There's a time limit.[20] You will have to accelerate, and acceleration is a huge energy user. Accelerating uphill is the biggest energy user of all. It's also the most fun. I'd be a better triathlete if I were a worse cyclist. But I'd be a middle-of-the-road triathlete either way, so I don't lose much sleep over it.[21]

I try to remember to eat and drink enough on the bike in the longer races. That's the place to do it. The swim is a little early for eating, not to mention inconvenient. While you're running, even if you're as

---

17 Still, it galls me just a little. I can't shake the vision of certain cyclists on more leisurely rides, good people all, who nonetheless park their bikes and go into a restaurant for lunch or spend an hour shopping without ever taking off their helmet. And my aerodynamic time trial helmet looks twice as goofy as theirs.

18 It also speeds me up before I get on the bike and slide into my shoes. Bare feet are a lot easier to run in than cycling shoes, especially on pavement. And if the transition zone isn't paved, bare feet have no cleats to fill up with sand, mud, or grass.

19 In most triathlons, once you're within 7 m of somebody, you're considered close enough to benefit from his or her draft and you have to pull through or drop back. That distance is a little startling to bike racers, who line up nose to stern like nothing so much as dogs making friends. To bike racers, a 1 m separation from the pack is a pink slip. On the other hand, a bike racer willing to get within a meter of a triathlete would be a little startling, too.

20 Fifteen seconds, which isn't so bad . . . the first couple of dozen times.

21 That's my story, and I've got the numbers to back it up.

smooth as a Kenyan on roller skates, there's enough bouncing around to make carrying large amounts of food and water as problematic as eating it, so you mostly sip what's available at the water stations. And by that point, anyway, you're just controlling the deficit. The bicycle is the true movable feast.[22] The bike holds and supports whatever you're drinking,

---

22 Though I don't think Hemingway mentions bikes in *A Moveable Feast*. But he writes about bike racers *having* a feast in *The Sun Also Rises*. He hardly mentions anything but boats and fishes and sharks and arm-wrestling in "The Old Man and the Sea," but for some reason that's the book I like to read before my toughest challenges.

and maybe what you're eating. Unless you've got it in your pockets, where it's still not bouncing around. You hardly notice any of it is there. Maybe that's the problem. If you get back to transition and notice a lot of your food and fluid *are* still there, you do have a problem.

I don't tend to whip through the transition zone as quickly from the bike to the run as I do from the swim to the bike, even though I don't have a wetsuit to squirm out of. Maybe it's because I've got one more pair of shoes to deal with plus socks to slide onto my sweaty feet. Maybe my gear has been kicked and scattered a little bit as others near me have moved through. Maybe it's just not a good time to hurry because things grow during the run. A little wrinkle in a sock grows for several miles until it's piano wire. Fluid and fuel left in the shade of the bike grow into a deficit of governmental proportions. Whatever lead I may have over some of my age-groupers . . . well, not everything grows during the run.

Right on schedule, my legs start griping that it's some other body part's turn to drive,[23] and sometimes I wish they'd protest a little harder, a little longer. Maybe that would help keep me from going out too fast. Yeah, that would be a plan. Like a funeral in the morning would make a person cheerier in the afternoon.

At least it would be a plan. One of my goals in this sport is to have a plan for the run and the wherewithal to execute it, but it usually boils down to survival and damage control and the keeping of promises. I can't even plan to give up on the plan properly because any good plan involves a surge, a kick, the discovery of reserves thought depleted, all of which—or at least enough of which—rise with the sound of the crowd and the first glimpse of the finish-line banner, and it's exactly the motivation I need to bring it home.

Unless it's one of those layouts where the race promoter sends everybody from the shadow of the banner to some wild-goose chase, some spur, a detour through a lab rat's labyrinth, or even around the far side and back again. Just like that, my motivation revolves entirely around a Captain Ahab–caliber thirst for vengeance, and if the promoters know what's good for them, they budgeted for some seriously distracting post-race refreshments.

I wish I could say what it feels like to cross the finish line, but I'm what the courts would call an unreliable witness. My story keeps changing. It's a happy feeling, but that's not specific and not exactly enlightening. I've been woozy a few times. I've come in fast enough to be shocked that I placed and slow enough to be relieved that I made it. I remember one race when my emotions bounced around like a ping-pong ball in a paint shaker, laughing and on the verge of tears and somehow watching it all from the side. I remember finishing one particularly scenic and brutal race so drained that I needed help walking, and still being disappointed that it was over. A lot of them, I can't even remember the part at the end. I'll have to do a hundred more races before I can establish any kind of usable pattern.

In fact, I'd love to do a hundred more. Maybe that's answer enough.

---

23   "Why not the appendix? The appendix never does *anything.*"

THE VIBE

riathlon can be a little like a religion, but it can be a whole lot like church. By "church" I specifically mean the First United Methodist Church I went to when I was a kid. By "a whole lot like church," I specifically mean the fourth Sunday of every month. That was Fellowship Sunday, which meant two services, six or eight hymns, two anthems, two doxologies, one and a half sermons, one half-a-sermon-long nap, one piercing wake-up glare from one's mother the organist, and finally that second benediction, followed by one enormous potluck dinner. In other words, a supreme test of endurance followed by a holy spread of carbohydrate-rich food, and if that doesn't sound like a triathlon, it *would* sound like one if bike saddles weren't so comfortable compared to wooden pews. I'll concede it's not a precise match. First Methodist didn't raffle off door prizes or even hand out goody bags, let alone medals or t-shirts. And the volunteers cleaning up after any given triathlon don't fight over who gets to run the vacuum cleaner the way Mr. Stafford[1] and Mr. Ostrander[2]

---

1   Not a real person.

128   2   Not a real person.

always did because they were convinced it cloaked certain side effects of Mrs. Gochanour's otherwise exemplary Round-up Beans.[3]

I don't know if churches do potlucks anymore in this day and age of foodborne illness fears and quieter vacuum cleaners. But we triathletes understand all about endurance, food, and fellowship.[4]

Other sports have their postcompetition social gatherings, to be sure. Golf has the Nineteenth Hole; Little League has the Dairy Queen; rugby has Alcoholics Anonymous. But I haven't found anything to rival the happy hour after a triathlon. It's not just the food, which can run the range from a few bagel halves and orange slices[5] to yogurt smoothies and greasy, nasty pizza.[6] What makes it work are the other athletes, a group of people separated by wildly divergent potentials and realities, united by a common task and a largely common goal, neither of which is brought any closer by stepping on someone else's good day.

Some of the faster racers will cross the finish line and take in a view of the transition zone, where other racers are still finishing their bike ride. The riders look back at them, and I daresay the exchange will be one of mutual respect, and before the day is done, they'll all be sitting around on the same grass with the same happy, tired buzz, kind of like Woodstock but with more naturopathic highs and better hair.[7]

---

3   A real casserole.

4   Although no one uses that word outside church and postgraduate studies.

5   Which, Spartan as that seems when you could have covered a used-car payment with your entry, beats the mayonnaise out of those summertime Fellowship Sundays, when it was just one damn potato salad after another.

6   Manna from heaven, as long as we're belaboring the church potluck theme. This puzzles newcomers and outsiders. Aren't triathletes health nuts who refuse to eat anything that isn't whole this or organic that or superfood-a-go-go, or at the very least served within five minutes of being picked? In a word: no. Well, maybe a few of us are, though the majority of that subset is a sub-subset that makes an exception after a race like a bishop on Fat Tuesday. Or the Indianapolis 500 driver chugging milk in the winner's circle, I suppose, but the Fat Tuesday simile is the more likely. The end of one race is but the start of preparations and deprivations for the next one, so we Mardi Gras it up. Plus, that stuff tastes so good if it catches you at the right time. And it doesn't get much righter than the moment your stomach settles after you've burned a few thousand calories. The quickest disappearing act I've seen performed by a menu item after a triathlon was a big load of the kind of hamburgers we Midwesterners poetically and perceptively christened sliders. They were gone by the time a dozen racers finished, though there were suspicions that they were consumed mostly by volunteers and even stronger suspicions that the overwhelming bulk of them were consumed by one volunteer in particular.

7   But, curiously, a lot of the same music.

They'll be talking about the race,[8] the weather,[9] their training,[10] their families,[11] their jobs,[12] the morning's peristaltic issues,[13] and their gear.[14] But they'll be as interested in everybody else's experience as they are eager to talk about their own.[15] Backs are patted; tips are traded; friends are made. Shoulders are a little sunburned, but people are too happy talking to care.

Like all good parties, it's all about the people and a bit about the food. Like all the *best* parties, the hosts go a little further. You'll arrive at the finish line to volunteers dispensing some combination of cold water; warm blankets; dry towels; icy sponges; a medal ranging from a lucky coin to Flavor Flav;[16] and a quick, thorough assessment of your ability to keep your body upright, your energy drink down,[17] and your eyes pointed in the same direction. They'll guide you, as necessary, to an ice bath, a medical professional, a massage table, or a discreet place to barf. I would not be surprised to learn that these volunteers receive marriage proposals, on the spot, on a regular basis.

I know.

I said "massage" and kept right on going. I'm circling back now.

Some race directors[18] will make an arrangement with a massage therapy college or clinic to have an army of therapists on hand for post-race massages. The upside for the triathletes is obvious enough, but it turns out the massage therapists like it pretty well, too. Professionals aren't going to be offered a more target-rich opportunity to promote themselves, and students get to spend the afternoon in the lab of all labs. Not

---

8   The hard parts, the easy parts, the hilly parts, the bumpy parts, the sunny parts, the shady parts, the windy parts, the part with the loose dog, the cold lake, and the hot corner marshal.

9   Ending with a shrug and a ". . . but what are you gonna do?"

10   Insufficient in retrospect, optimistic looking ahead.

11   Who are often sitting right there as well.

12   Actually, not so much their jobs.

13   With a frankness and fervor not otherwise seen outside nursing homes.

14   Always gear.

15   Except regarding the peristalsis.

16

17   If you haven't gone and looked up "peristalsis" yet, now you don't need to.

18   I say "some race directors" in the same tone of voice I use when I refer to the works of David Mamet as "some plays."

only is the supply of patients close to endless, they actually tend to have identifiable muscles beneath a much thinner layer of, ah, tissue[19] than the population at large[20] has to offer. Our sweaty, fragrant, slimy skin, I'm told, is a small price to pay for the opportunity.

Everybody loves the massage therapists, but they're hardly the only professionals and Potential New Best Friends hanging around the place. Let's start with the bike-shop tent. As, indeed, a lot of people do. Sooner or later,[21] you're going to arrive at a race and realize you've forgotten something crucial—your goggles, a water bottle, some energy gel, a spare tube, a tire pump, or a minimally functional amount of lubricant on your chain. A couple of guys in cutoff shorts and grease-stained aprons will be there to cheerfully lift your bike onto the stand and set you, or your wobbly rim, straight. Or they'll fill your tires to the proper pressure and maybe even recommend a few adjustments for the course and conditions, like a good golf caddy but without the pressure to tip.[22] If it's merchandise you need, like the goggles or the food or the clever, boastful t-shirt,[23] they'll sell that to you as well.[24]

There may be physical therapists or chiropractors or other wellness pros there, offering you a chance to sample their skills or take home a pen or a calendar or some sticky notes.

There might also be a team of race photographers posted at key points around the course, capturing every racer possible as many times as possible[25] and posting their wares for sale as soon as they can get them onto a Web site.

---

19   We're being subtle here.

20   But not very subtle.

21   Generally sooner, though I am qualified to say that novices have the forgetfulness market far from cornered.

22   Although this is a concept worth pondering.

23   Much more optional than crucial, but it doesn't always seem that way at the time.

24   A word of caution: They will invariably display something new that you've always been tempted to try, and by "something" I mean "energy drink or food." This is not the time to try those things. Buy it afterward and give it a go in training, but race day is not the time to serve your stomach a surprise. Because for as many gels and bars and drinks and chews as I see for sale *before* the race, I have never seen Kaopectate available *during* the race.

25   These shooters are pros, and they'll do their very best to make you look good. But they can be thwarted. I get them on the run. I look pretty good on the bike and okay, if a pupil-constricting shade of Norwegian, coming out of the water and peeling off my wetsuit. But in all the years I've been racing, I have never, ever taken a good photo running. I look like that guy Edvard Munch painted in *The Scream*. I would look like death if you took my picture while I was running across the living room to hug Miss July. I don't know why. My low point was a photo shot at the Musselman, a half-Ironman in New York's Finger Lakes region.

Or there may not be any of those folks. Some races are a little like festivals and expos, some resemble a high-stakes championship,[26] and some just look like a bunch of guys getting together to back up some old boasts.[27] Whatever your taste and whatever the level of marketing and distractions around the start-finish area, there's one guy at every race who's everybody's instant friend, walking across the grass trailing supplicants like Leonard Nimoy at a *Star Trek* convention. He's the guy heading over to post the results.

Because for a sport that's all about individual effort, individual goals, individual triumph, and individual drama, we're all awfully interested in how our individual effort compares to everybody else's individual effort.

I mean, you can only talk about gear and weather for so long.

The run begins and ends lakeside, so when I saw a shot of myself looking especially cadaverous with the lake off to my left, at least I knew I'd earned the look. I showed it to Brian, my friend and training partner and reality check supremo. "This is what a real effort looks like after 12.8 miles," I said. And Brian said, "If there's a quarter mile to go, isn't the lake supposed to be on your right?" Oh.

26 Which, duh, some of them *are* high-stakes championships.

27 And some are fiascos. It happens in triathlon just as it does in any other business. Best you can do is be wary; check what more experienced racers say; and if that doesn't work, apply the "Fool me twice, shame on me . . ." rule.

CHAPTER 1

What We've Learned About Our Resources

THE MONEY

Some economists divide the world into *Haves* and *Have-Nots*. Just as an example, there are a few economists who *Have* jobs after espousing such an oversimplified crock of hooey, and a whole bunch more who *Have Not*. And it is a crock of hooey. Look at this—right away, it gets more complicated. What about people who say such things and Have a job, but the job is in talk radio or triathlon-book writing and Not in anything that substantially improves our society?

That's why I'm much more comfortable oversimplifying the world through a different lens, dividing the world into *Did*s and *Did Not*s. You either Did a triathlon or you Did Not. *Did*s are immediately subdivided into *Did One and That's It* and *Did One and Want More*; *Did Not*s split into *Did Not and Won't* and *Did Not Yet but Will*. *Did One and That's It*s get further subdivided into *Did One and Moved on to the Next Adventure* and *Did One and Returned to the Big-Butt Chair in Front of the Television and the Hell with It*, whereas *Did One and Want More*s get split into *Let's Have This Enhance My Life* and *Let's Allow This to Take over My Life*. Those are further split and nuanced while others circumvent the whole mess and join back up on the flip side, like the way *Did One and Want More* and *Did Not Yet but Will* merge to form my favorite category, *Bring It On*. But I'm afraid if I get into it too deeply, someone's going to send me to business school, where I will have to cut back on my training and racing and wear a sport coat and still won't know a thing about economics.[1]

Here's to the *Bring It Ons*. They've discovered and accepted the rare axiom economists do tend to agree on, namely, that nothing of value is free. And if economists don't agree that the inverse, that no effort goes unrewarded, is true, it's only because they need to do some triathlons themselves.

The *Bring It Ons* have an idea of the price, of what it takes to do a triathlon; the *Did One and Want More* subset has seen it firsthand, and the *Did Not Yet but Will* subset knows enough that perhaps that's why they've been putting it off. So let's talk about the inverse. Let's talk about what you get.

And to really keep me out of the Department of Economics, I'll go straight to money and make the outrageous assertion that this sport of expensive featherweight bikes and expensive rubber suits and expensive shoes you're forever replacing and expensive entry fees and the obligatory $2 "I Tri"[2] bumper sticker for each car is actually *saving you money*.

Outrageous assertion explanation, basic: Every dollar you spend on triathlon gear and entry fees is a dollar you're not wasting on alcohol, cigarettes, video games, bad food, dreadful art,[3] heroin, premium cable channels you never watch anyway, the water bill, single-dollar-bill "tips," gambling, golf, and vacations where all the restaurants are recognizable franchises.[4]

Outrageous assertion explanation, slightly more nuanced (since the basic version assumes you're part of the vast herd of Americans who never save any money, and that might not be correct): Forget about the money.

---

1 Not that that seems to be a big obstacle in economics. I'm not saying I'm smarter than an economist, but nobody's story checks out with the next guy's. When you've got that many experts disagreeing on so many fundamental levels, you just know there's at least a 12-pack of bogus Nobels out there.

2 Or "140.6," or "70.3," or the little stick figures of the three sports; whatever it takes to assure the world that the scuff marks on the roof didn't come from just any old rack.

3 This is a nod to art critic, teacher, and all-around bon vivant Dr. Green, partly because he's a dear friend but mostly because I've been waiting for years to fit "bon vivant" into something I wrote.

4 Gambling, golf, and that kind of vacation *can* be redundant, but they aren't *necessarily* redundant, and anyway, I wouldn't want to give the impression that I was ruling out, say, the entire state of Florida.

If you're using all that new triathlon stuff the right way, you won't even have time to go shopping for bad art and heroin.

Outrageous assertion explanation well worth considering: Being healthy is a lot cheaper than being sick. Although governments and businesses and workers and unions and columnists and doctors and insurance companies argue ad nauseam[5] about every other aspect of health care, the one thing everybody seems to agree on is that healthy people are a bargain[6] compared to unhealthy people.[7] I'm sorry I can't give you specific numbers

---

5   That even sounds like a medical term, doesn't it?
6   Like a Picasso at a garage sale.
7   Like a hundred-grand paint-by-number.

because there's not a straight number to be had from the aforementioned crowd. If you're not inclined to take my word without documentation, keep this discussion in mind for a few weeks. Read the paper, cruise the Internet, watch the news, look at drug-company ads, whatever. It won't take long for someone to mention health care costs, and then it shouldn't take long for them to toss out one of the endlessly varying numbers associated with a certain condition. Write that number down and just see how many bikes, helmets, wetsuits, running shoes, entry fees, and[8] articles of clothing you can buy for the price of, say, a trip to the emergency room with chest pains. Is chest pain a little dramatic? Okay. Joint replacement. Type 2 diabetes. Cholesterol and blood-pressure drugs. You can buy a lot of toys with what you're not spending on that stuff.

There are no guarantees in life, of course. Bad fortune finds us all, and even the healthiest of us can find ourselves smote with something a healthy lifestyle couldn't prevent after all. A year before I wrote this, I had surgery to shore up two, count 'em, two hernias. The noble and virtuous lifestyle of a middle-aged, middling-proficiency triathlete apparently couldn't deflect that. But I was an easy patient. Good health in general meant I wasn't getting in the way of my own healing process.[9] And my he-man triathlete tolerance for pain meant I could sell every last one of my Percocets on the black market and buy myself a cool new "Dopers Suck" jersey.[10]

Outrageous assertion explanation that acknowledges that the rest of the world is even more outrageous, so you might as well cash in on it: Every so often the story pops up that skinny people get hired faster for better jobs.[11] Is that fair? Probably not. Is it believable? Absolutely. Is it to triathletes' advantage if it's so? (Shrug.) And is it totally outrageous even as we acknowledge its patent unfairness? Triathletes are by nature goal-oriented, efficient, enthusiastic, confident, and happy, and who wouldn't want a workplace full of that?[12] Your thin profile may just be a secondary trait that gets noticed first.

---

8   Note the "and." Not "or." "And."

9   This is a minor exaggeration. I did get in the way of my own healing process, and it was triathlon's fault. After you have an operation like that, they won't let you go home until you pee. That would have been a nice thing to know before I dehydrated myself a bit with a swim and a soak in a hot tub the day before the operation.

10 This, on the other hand, is wholly false, an ill-advised play for a cheap laugh. That said, I really didn't need anything stronger than ibuprofen.

11 Tall people, too, but all the training in the world can't help some of us there.

12 That funny way we walk the early part of the week after a tough long-course race notwithstanding.

So look at all the money you're saving by spending money. Yeah. It's like we're in a comic strip from the 1950s, Blondie prancing through Tudbury's department store while Dagwood straggles behind balancing the day's savings piled so high that all you can see is that bizarre trademark haircut. This rationale is fun, but it has its limits. You don't want to blow the kid's college tuition on a $6,000 bike.

But getting every last cent's worth out of a $2,000 bike and being able to walk effortlessly across campus at her graduation whispers "bargain" all over again.

THE SMARTS

Triathlon makes you smarter.

I don't know if it makes you smart in an absolute sense because nobody really knows what smart is. The first ape-man to make use of a sharpened stick was the smartest creature on Earth. I know this from reading *2001: A Space Odyssey*, which was written by Arthur C. Clarke, who would also make a viable candidate for the smartest creature on Earth, and he probably couldn't fend off a lethargic armadillo with an M-16.

So whatever smart is, it's not absolute. It must be relative. But relative to whom? You'll always be dumber than whoever invented the Oreo cookie.[1] But you'll always be smarter than the bank robber who writes the stickup note on the back of his deposit slip.[2]

---

1   Really, is there a more perfect food? Even if it's probably not technically actual food?

2   This happens so often it doesn't even make the news anymore on its own. Nowadays, if you want to get any coverage, you have to write your stickup note on the back of your deposit slip and hand it over while wearing a "Hi, I'm Willie Sutton, and I'll be your bank robber today" pin.

Not to mention, you can be really smart and really dumb at the same time. Galileo was smart enough to prove that the sun didn't revolve around the Earth and dumb enough to tell the pope.

I believe the best we can hope for is to be smarter than we were before. Which, if you start with a low enough point of reference, is easy. I was named Most Improved Rider my rookie year of racing bicycles with the mighty Rapid Wheelmen. It's not that I was terribly good by my final race of the year. It had more to do with my first race of the year, in which I crashed spectacularly. In a roller race,[3] in the middle of a shopping mall. After that, Most Improved Rider was mine to lose.

With that in mind, remember that you begin a triathlon by jumping into a large body of water that may be any combination of cold, rough, and crowded, and then tell me if you aren't destined to get a whole lot smarter than that by the time the swim is over.

Ha, ha. It's more long-term than that. Sometimes it takes until after you've been on the bike long enough to dry off and warm up.

Ha, ha. It's a lot more long-term than *that*. It's a lifetime quest. It can take decades of this stuff before you notice you've done anything smart at all, and by that point it starts to feel like wisdom. Both of which, smarts and wisdom,[4] it has to be said, can seem rather counterintuitive products of a sport that's mostly a matter of spending a long time traveling in a straight line at something less than top speed in a steady state of discomfort. Sort of like . . . college. How about that? I think I just said something wise.

Besides, this sport is richer in facts than you might think. I'll give you just a few. Take notes[5] because there's a follow-up question. Okay: You learn you have limits. You learn what they are.[6] You learn that they change from event to event, from day to day, from year to year. You learn that your limits are as real as they are changeable, and that short-term

---

3   To be fair, you do have to balance your bike on the rollers, and it can seem kind of tricky. But there's what's fair and there's what's true, and this is what's true: Crashing an exercise bike is crashing an exercise bike.

4   Smarts is like cash. Wisdom is like your retirement annuity. Beyond that is philosophy, which is like default swaps and credit derivatives, something so complicated and arcane that people just pretend it's significant even if it turns out to be bullshit. The great philosopher Friedrich Nietzsche, just to use an example that happens to be popular with triathletes, said that whatever didn't kill him made him stronger. But would it have killed him to shave off that ridiculous mustache? Would it have made him stronger?

5   Better yet, mark up the book with a highlighter pen and then buy another, virgin copy for company to read. (Apparently another thing you learn from triathlon is the power of marketing.)

6   Or at least you get a better idea.

stubbornness on race day will get you closer to them, but only long-term stubbornness throughout the year will move them farther from where you are.

You learn that there are two types of people who don't get pummeled during the swim: the guy in the very front and everybody who figures out that it's worth the extra 10 feet to swim a little wide and avoid the scrum. You learn that relaxing makes you swim faster than just trying harder. You learn that wetsuits are tight and a little awkward to remove and that swim trunks have a drawstring for a reason. You learn in the transition zone that going through a mental checklist is a lot faster than thinking, no matter how fast you think and how much of your gear your clumsy, vertiginous neighbor kicked away from where the checklist says to look for it.

You learn that wind resistance increases by the square of velocity, and that every mile per hour you ride your bike below that speed, the more you waste your money on aerodynamic equipment, and every mile per hour above that speed, the more you waste your strength on a part of the race that's still nowhere near the finish line. And that the more money and strength you have in the first place, the less the waste matters. You learn that a $2,000 disc wheel can make less difference than a $1.50 packet of energy gel. That officials really are watching to see if you're drafting, and that even if[7] they're wrong, they're in charge.[8] You learn that you can't win a triathlon with a good bike ride alone, but you can lose it with a bad one.

You learn that sore muscles at the beginning of the run sometimes work themselves out but irritations closer to the surface only get worse. That it's worth figuring out in advance what brands of socks slide on most smoothly over sweaty feet. That you're having a pretty good race if spectators are yelling how many people are how many seconds in front of you; you're having an okay race if they're yelling, "You can do it"; and you're maybe not in line for a personal record if you hear one telling another, "If he can do it, I can do it." You learn that you can't win a triathlon with a good run alone, but you can ruin it with a bad one, and that the best way to lose the race on the run is to try to win the race on the bike or in the water.

Pencils down. Quiz time. What did all those facts have in common? Same thing the triathlon events themselves have in common. They all look specific on the surface, but they can all, with the tiniest of modifications, be applied to each other and to life in general.

---

7   Rather, when.
8   And that habitual, egregious drafters learn exactly what certain motorcycles sound like at bicycle speed.

Swimming relaxed is faster than panicking? Right. And running relaxed is faster than banging your head against the wall, too. Same with cycling. And same with getting through rush-hour traffic or a master's thesis.

On your bike, you very quickly learn how different levels of effort squander different resources. Of course. We could all use a little balance in our swimming, our running, and our lives.

That wrinkled sock inside your running shoe that felt tolerable for the first half mile and has you all but gangrenous by the fifth mile is a nice refutation of "don't sweat the small stuff" that can just as easily apply to a misadjusted shifter, a leaky goggle, or the dentist's appointment that's so easy to put off.

Still, isolated facts like that, however transferable and relevant, fade next to the fact that this sport simply makes you think. A lot. About logical stuff, about weird stuff, about stuff that never seems to go anywhere. And just like exercise, if you think enough about anything, you'll get a little better at everything.

There was a newspaper columnist in Chicago a while ago[9] named Sydney J. Harris who would regularly devote an installment to something along the lines of "Things I Learned en Route to Looking Up Other Things." I loved that feature, and I loved that concept, and I wonder if it's largely lost in a time when you can get a question answered pretty much instantly and directly[10] via some Internet search engine.[11]

You can find triathlons in Google, but there's no Google in triathlon. You can't download red blood cells. You can't click through to the finish line. You can look up just how much water you need to drink, but the notion won't stick until you get it right a few times, and you won't get it right until you get it wrong twice as many times as that. If you want to learn how to swim without your feet sinking, you have to get into the pool and practice. And if, in the process, you learn how to keep your elbows high at the same time, well, Sydney J. Harris would be proud. And if you learn that the best lanes are available at five in the morning and on the way there you rediscover how beautiful the sunrise looks, I'll be proud. And when you learn that the lifeguards are only too happy to turn on the water slide in the empty splash pool and that it's a silly, self-indulgent joy of a way to end a workout and start a day, why, then, my work is done. You can't get much smarter than that.

---

9   Long enough ago to have been on the Master List of Nixon's Political Opponents. How cool is that?

10   And sometimes even accurately.

11   Although, ironically, good luck finding and confirming the exact damn title of Sydney J. Harris's "Things I Learned . . ." feature.

THE DISCIPLINE

We'd better talk about sex here.

Sex and discipline.[1] Not because they necessarily go together[2] but because no one is otherwise going to voluntarily read about discipline.

Also because sex and discipline have a lot in common. One thing in common, anyway, but it's a biggie: You notice it most when you've gone without it for a while.

Furthermore, sex and discipline tend to be highly and widely recommended, although the pattern is for people to highly recommend the one for themselves and the other for everybody else. And hence the two

---

1   This should be good, from a guy who restricts himself to a gazillion footnoted digressions per chapter.

2   Turns out they do if you look in the right sections of the right kind of shops in the right parts of the right cities, which you'll know by how many people call them the "wrong" ones. (Don't go into that part of the shop. Not because it's sinful or deviant but because way too much of the clothing looks like something you paid twice as much for at the triathlon store.)

begin to split, the way an amoeba might split through mitosis. Mitosis is a cellular-level method of reproduction in which cells split into two identical daughter cells. It is neither sexual nor disciplined, nor is it especially exciting,[3] which is fine with me because it puts all this discipline discussion into a more tolerable perspective.

Discipline. If you ask me, it gets a bad rap, all drill-sergeant this and self-denial that. *Webster's Collegiate Dictionary* doesn't help, defining the word first as simply PUNISHMENT, following up with a number of equally fascist-sounding words and phrases, and finally pulling out the good stuff all the way down at definition 5c: SELF-CONTROL.

Webster's lexicographers should have put SELF-CONTROL first. But they didn't,[4] so we will. Suddenly discipline doesn't sound so bad. When you take a cold look at modern life and tote up just how much of it you spend at the mercy of other people and their needs and whims and demands, the idea of having a little of your own control over yourself sounds a little more complex and a lot more appealing. It starts to sound more like living life on your own terms, your own way. This is discipline I can get behind.

When my wife and I decided to get married,[5] we decided to have our wedding in a church even though religion wasn't a looming presence in either of our lives. Part of the reason was that church did loom large in both our families' lives.[6] I think the rest had to do with the stained-glass windows. But the church had certain conditions. The minister got to spend one afternoon before the wedding telling us how not to get divorced in the 50 or so years afterward. One afternoon isn't much, but the reverend was efficient. He didn't size us up as lushes or cheats or people who make their living in motion pictures, so he zeroed in on the thought that maybe our biggest threat would be money, and just like that, he was done sounding like a minister at all. He sounded like a financial adviser, and a pretty good one.

I don't remember as much as I'm supposed to about my wedding,[7] but I remember what he told us about money during Marriage Lessons: to pay ourselves first. To invest a good chunk of every paycheck, without fail, before we paid any bills, bought any groceries, or indulged in any toys. We'd find a way to take care of those other essentials, but if we didn't do it in that order, we wouldn't invest, we wouldn't build up any kind

---

3   Maybe it would be more exciting if amoeba shopped in the right sections of the right kind of shops in the right parts of the right cities.

4   And for that they should be punished!

5   Marriage? So we're done talking about sex, then?

6   If anyone understands what I was getting at in the previous paragraph about other people controlling things, it's youngsters getting married.

7   I'm a guy.

of reserve, we'd always be worried about money, and we'd eventually get divorced and never get to retire.[8]

He said to be disciplined.

Really. Giving yourself money was discipline.

Well, hell. If a lesson is worth learning, it's worth transferring. And the day I won my age group for the first time, I wanted to send the reverend a big bunch of flowers.[9]

Because if it's considered disciplined to pay yourself your own money, then it's got to be disciplined to take care of yourself in other areas, too.

---

8   The joke's on him. I'm a writer and a cartoonist, so I'll never be able to retire anyway. Or divorce. Benefits, you know.

9   Or perhaps my winnings, but I don't know what he would have done with a wooden plaque the size of a playing card that had a picture of three athletes on it and nothing else.

Areas like your physical and mental health. By paying yourself your own *time*, and investing it in racing and training. And just as we found ways to pay the grocer and the mortgage banker and everybody else who was pretty sure they had first whack at our paycheck, so I can stick to a training plan and still do right by everybody who's pretty sure my time is his or her property.[10]

That's the discipline I learned elsewhere and applied to triathlon. I think I learned even more discipline from triathlon and applied it everywhere else. See, once you give yourself the time to race and train, there's a certain duty, or at least desire, to do it right. And triathlon is, at its heart, a perseverance contest.[11]

You have to persevere when it hurts. Whether it's the dull, pervasive throb at the end of an Ironman, the lactic acid burn in a sprint, or the knife in the gut[12] as you close out a set of anaerobic intervals,[13] you persevere. You persevere because that's what you showed up to do. You persevere because you owe it to some of the people who have to wait while you pay yourself first. You persevere because you don't want to quit and step onto that slippery slope.[14] You persevere because, as Robert Frost said, "The best way out is always through," and even though he was purportedly a nasty old fart[15] who wouldn't have known a shin splint from Shinola, nobody ever said a more apt thing about racing triathlons.

You have to persevere when it doesn't hurt, and that's harder. Before you have to tango with your limits, you have to make it to the dance. That kind of restraint is a little tough on certain personalities, say, mine. And once you've learned to go fast when it hurts, it takes some serious discipline to go slow when you're comfortable.

The weird thing is, discipline itself doesn't seem to have a whole lot of self-control. It's all over the place. You save your money, prices go up.

---

10   Let's not get the idea that my life is perfect. When one of us lost our job, my wife and I didn't pay ourselves quite as much and could very easily have ended up going through a stretch when we didn't pay ourselves at all. And sometimes, in my deadline-oriented business, I do have to put other obligations first. This is not a disaster when we've been behaving all along and have built up a reserve. That's the idea. What it really is, though, is another discovery: You can put yourself first, or you can put the world first, and the world doesn't bitch about it any more or any less either way.

11   In the longer events, it's also an eating contest, but not at its heart. Closer to the duodenum.

12   Good God. Aren't we quite the drama queen here?

13   When no one is looking, you helpfully remind yourself.

14   Especially in cycling shoes.

15   Also, he wrote his own epitaph. His tombstone reads, "I had a lover's quarrel with the world."

You persevere, you get better at racing; you get better, you enter tougher races that require more perseverance. But with triathlon, as with money, the outcome tends to shake out in your favor in the long term. I don't know why it works that way with money,[16] but I know why it does with triathlon: memory.

Whatever the pain, whatever the difficulty, whatever the pressure from the world's me-first types who don't get it, whatever the obstacle, every time you suffer through it is one more time you realize you can. *"What the hell?"* becomes *"Oh, this again."*

A pharmacist friend told me once that "narcotic painkiller" was a bit of an oxymoron. "Narcotics don't make the pain go away," he said. "You're still in pain. You just don't care."

So there you go. Let me be the first to associate discipline with opium. Since associating it with sex didn't really go anywhere.

16   I mean, really. You read my chapter on economics.

CHAPTER 2

What We've Learned About Our Bodies

FUEL

I never quite understood why Pride was one of the Seven Deadly Sins. Not because Pride is without its downside,[1] and not because it does seem to have as many or more upsides, but simply because, either way, it's got the lifespan of a hypertensive mayfly.

Case in point, and one that brings us back into the supposed subject matter of this book:[2] All this triathlon stuff I do makes me pretty proud of myself. I'm proud of my accomplishments; I'm proud of the work ethic training and racing have taught me; I'm proud of the way I feel; and, okay, I'll come right out and admit it, I'm proud of the way I look for a guy my age. All this pride seems justified, or at least earned. It feels good. And

---

1   In that we all know too many people who fall under the category of Asshole and Proud of It. But then it needs to be asked: Is the sin Pride, or is the sin Being an Asshole? Because if they made the latter a sin, you could pretty much boil the list of seven right down to one and be done with it.

2   If not, quite yet, the subject matter of this chapter section.

I enjoy it fully and guiltlessly, safe in the knowledge that the world will not let me sustain the emotion long enough to do any real sinful damage.

Case in point within a case in point: Midway through a long drive home from a disastrous half-Ironman, I stopped for a sandwich, soup, and coffee. I was still thrashed from the race and figured I looked it. But maybe not. It appeared that the hottie behind the counter was interested in more than my order. She was . . . was she? . . . She was *checking me out!* I was gaunt and exhausted, but by God, I was lean and fit and still had it going on. Pride. Pause. "Are you . . ." she leaned toward me, ". . . Tiffany's dad?"

And that was that for Pride, which was just as well since there didn't seem to be any other Deadly Sins going on in the vicinity to keep it company.

Thank God for small favors. Because it's even worse when we do inspire impure thoughts and they turn out to be the wrong ones. I can handle that I'm a few years beyond inspiring Lust. I'm happy to fill people with Envy, except that what people seem to covet in me is yet another vice: Gluttony.[3]

"You are *sooooo* lucky!" I'm informed. "With all that exercise,[4] you must get to eat *all the time!*" It's an impression that's not altogether groundless, but neither is it altogether complete. There's the twin issue of also getting to be hungry all the time.

Being constantly hungry in America is like being a randy sailor on shore leave in Amsterdam. Being a constantly hungry serious endurance athlete is like being in Amsterdam with your mom. Treasures abound. Options are sparse.

I overstate. In spite of our modern abundance of, and reliance on, all things processed and packaged, any given supermarket has a fresh produce section to make you feel like a Lilliputian rolling around in Gulliver's salad bowl,[5] year-round, unencumbered by antiquities like growing seasons.

It's truly amazing. The supermarket can bring fresh grapes all the way from Chile—*Chile!*—and sell them to you for $1 a pound if you catch the right sale. Even more amazing is how many of us opt instead for the peanut-butter cups by the cash register, at more like $8 a pound for the name-brand ones.

---

3   Now we're on topic.

4   Have you ever noticed the difference between the people who call it "exercise" and the people who call it "training"? It's like there's a secret password, isn't it?

5   "Waiter! What's this triathlete doing in my gazpacho?" "Freestyle, sir. Triathletes can't backstroke."

Oh, see, I'm doing it again. I'm using a sensational example for effect. *We're* not buying peanut-butter cups at $8 a pound. We're triathletes. *We're* buying packets of gel. At closer to $20 a pound.

I'm in no position to criticize. I'm old enough[6] to remember the days before gels and bars and any powder but Kool-Aid and Tang. I've had pockets bulging with grapes and stained with juice. I've finished rides smelling of wet wool and banana peel. I can remember when Hitting the Wall was the crux of the marathon before somebody figured out you could carry

---

6   Ask Tiffany's friend behind the counter at the restaurant.

the nutritional component of your second wind with you.[7] And I like it better the modern way.

All this high-priced, highly hyped, foil-wrapped nutrition is a gift from heaven.[8] If I had to choose between the technological leaps in carbon fiber and carbohydrates, I wouldn't have to ponder long.

I buy tons of that stuff, and I've tried more. Bars, gels, and now gumdrop-like chews; mixes for fuel and others for recovery; capsules full of electrolytes—all of it. Some sit better than the others, some sort of work, some are counterproductive, and some work so well I'm almost afraid to use them lest I actually win something and have to wonder if, you know, it wasn't really me.

Or if it wasn't really the marketing. Make no mistake, this stuff is pitched to us as heavily and shamelessly as Fructose Flakes and Diabete-Os are during Saturday-morning cartoons.

And then there are the contradictions. There's Lon Haldeman in the 1980s, rewriting the book on endurance cycling en route from McDonald's to McDonald's. There are journeyman elite racers living in their cars and subsisting on Pop-Tarts. There's the way the food tables by the finish line run out of cookies before they run out of orange slices. And then there's the one that really got my attention. The *International Journal of Sport Nutrition and Exercise Metabolism*[9] published a study that said chocolate milk can hold its own with any specialty recovery drink.

Now, here was a busted myth I could get behind. Junk food as performance fuel. Vice as virtue. There was a twentieth-century author and critic, Edward Dahlberg, who didn't know that much about nutrition,[10] who noted famously that "what most men desire is a virgin who is a whore."[11] Chocolate milk was the nutritional equivalent of Dahlberg's notion. A marketing firm tasked with getting people to buy more milk jumped all over that one and maybe got a wee bit overenthusiastic with its claims. A company that sold a lot of sports drink jumped right back, and

---

7   In 1986, I finished a 24-hour bike race largely on diluted apple juice and a couple of thousand bananas softened into caulk inside my jersey pocket. Also in 1986, a runner named Brian Maxwell and his wife were experimenting on their kitchen stove with a sugary glop that they thought might help fuel him through marathons. In 2000, the Maxwells sold PowerBar to Nestlé, and I was just getting around to eating bananas again.

8   Or from Berkeley. I can't imagine one is a whole lot different from the other.

9   Whoa. A magazine with a title like that sure begs for a big, fat footnote without leaving much for the footnote to say. So I will say this: You sure don't see a lot of copies of the *International Journal of Sport Nutrition and Exercise Metabolism* on the higher shelves at the barbershop.

10   But had a lot to say about sex; he wasn't stupid.

11   Lust! I'm not the only one beating the sin theme to death.

the fight was on. Suddenly the atmosphere was more Jell-O[12] Wrestling Nite than endurance sports nutrition research. The poor Indiana University professor who did the study in the first place was left to wonder why everybody missed the larger point that the real benefit was in consuming *anything* at all nutritious right after a workout.

Common sense, in other words.

If sense comes from trial and error, I have to believe that common sense comes from common trial and common error—"common" as in "plentiful." And triathletes are all about plenty. Our lives are a cornucopia of trials and errors as we constantly search for balance: between fuel and ballast, between what tastes good and what works,[13] between what's whole and natural and resembles something that came from the land instead of a factory and what can be reasonably prepared between the end of a hard day's training and the beginning of a hard night's sleep. We experiment as a by-product of sheer volume because we burn and replace calories like a steel foundry.[14] The demand is daunting, but the excess is forgiving. That much food is simply going to contain a lot of nutrients if you put any effort at all into your choices.

Food science degree optional. I attended a college of such a size and during such an era that some of the coaches apparently had to teach a class or two[15] as well as coaching. And by "a" class, I of course mean the generic and required health class. Life was good. If anything sounded more promising than watching the stereotypical whistle-on-a-lanyard coach try to lecture about, say, human sexuality,[16] it was having one of

---

12 No endorsement expressed or implied, nor any claim that plain old applesauce is any better or worse a medium for women to fight in for the entertainment of guys who are doing their own unsuccessful research into the slimming effects of light beer.

13 Which are often one and the same. It's hard for your tissues to absorb even the best superfood if you can't get it past your uvula.

14 A friend of mine, a talented bicycle racer, traveled to Belgium a few springs ago to watch some of the classics like Paris-Roubaix and the Tour of Flanders. These are high-profile, high-stakes, winner-take-all dogfights played out over brutally rough terrain in often dreadful weather. He stood on the shoulder of the narrow road in the middle of however you say nowhere in Flemish and watched the leaders, then the peloton, then the stragglers, fly by. He was awestruck by the speed and the strength of the riders, but he was expecting to be. "What surprised me," he said, "was the heat coming off them."

15 !

16 Without question a high point of the semester. Class halted for about five minutes so we could regain some semblance of composure after he pronounced "fallopian tubes" to sound like "Pheidippian tubes" too many times. (I'm guessing about 26.2 times, but that's just a guess.)

his assistant coaches substitute for him and talk about nutrition.[17] But damned if the assistant coach didn't get it right, if on a simple level. "I just try to put as many different colors of food on my plate as I can," he said, "and then make sure there ain't anything left over when I'm done."

I thought I was in the presence of genius. I don't know if he could ever get that published in the *International Journal of Sport Nutrition and Exercise Metabolism*, but I decided right then and there that it sounded like a pretty good approach to life in general.

You are what you eat. Right?

---

17 It was like having Yogi Berra fill in for Casey Stengel. In *Hamlet*.

DURABILITY

Triathlon has given me a good life, but it ruined a good line.

I was a kid, say, around 20, hang gliding above a popular Northern Michigan ridge when I caught some stereotypically Northern Michigan weather. There were maybe eight of us surfing a mellow onshore breeze as it flowed over a 400-foot bluff when Lake Michigan had a mood swing and it was time to land in a hurry. The nearest landing zone was five miles down the shore, and we fought our way there through a smorgasbord of cold, gusty, swirling, vulgar air[1] to an uncharitable sliver of beach where we had to come in hot, unclip quickly, and get the hell out of the way so the next puckered pilot could bring it in. One guy, who must have been pushing 40, got his butt out of the cauldron, his rig out of the landing zone, and his life out of the balance and said the funniest thing. He said, "I'm too old for this shit." Hilarious![2]

---

1   A buffet of buffeting, as it were.

2   I know. You had to be there. You had to be standing there shivering not from the cold, sideways rain but from something a little deeper, the realization that any flight, anything at all, any day, could have you a few minutes from The End, and that that's about as old as you're ever going to get. (NB: I didn't *say* it was "Life in These United States" funny.)

Right then I started looking forward to the day when I would be old enough to use that line, and then I ruined it all by racing triathlons. I'm older now than that pilot in the rain was then, but I'm younger than a lot of the guys who train with me and race with me and don't always wait up for me. We enter races and split into age groups[3] that, by the time we're even out of the water, seem as arbitrary as lining up according to hair color.[4] We don't get older.[5] We "age up." Every five years, we eagerly cross over into a new age group, figuring that maybe this is the year we can win some medals, only to discover that we're racing against the same guys, but now they're more experienced, too.

Too old for this shit? I'm still not old enough.

I guess triathlon is one of those lifetime sports, whatever that means. I used to think it meant any sport but football, which you can't do when you're old, and shuffleboard, which you can't do when you're young. But I think it just means that if you're like a lot of triathletes, you get hooked on it and want to do it for a very long time, so you'd better take care of yourself.

Taking care of yourself is no small order in a sport that involves so much repetitive stress. How many times a week does a runner ask the small bones in his or her legs and feet to absorb the impact of a body's weight and subsequently, immediately, launch the same mass forward? How much is the tiniest misalignment magnified over hours of spinning at 100 rpm, or mashing at 70 rpm? How many times a year can you work a job and a family around a training plan that demands the equivalent of a part-time job? How early do you have to get up to train right and still be home in time to get the kids off to school?[6] How much sleep can you sacrifice to accommodate a regimen that turns right around and increases your need for sleep?

I could make a good case that it works because an endurance sport like triathlon teaches pacing. There are no medals if you don't finish.[7] But I've smelled too much muscle cream and coffee breath during group

---

3   You've heard the expression that age is just a number? In this sport, it's not even a number, it's a range. "How old is Brian?" my wife will ask. "Fifty to 54," I will answer in all seriousness.

4   Gray, in my case. In a lot of cases. I may have chosen a bad example.

5   Yes, we do. We age and we recognize it, but it's different and it's weird. I finally acknowledged, only recently, that I'm not only middle-aged but solidly, undeniably so. The epiphany didn't happen while I was looking backward through any wistful glory-days nonsense. It happened when I was looking forward. I was setting goals, and I had decided I would aim to qualify for the Boston Marathon when I turned 50 to 54. And I realized that it was a short-term goal.

6   Or, for that matter, yourself off to work.

7   Perhaps more significantly, there are no refunds if you don't start.

workouts[8] to claim any kind of majority has that figured out. Clearly we're not enduring out of any sense of restraint.

Or maybe triathlon teaches us something even more profound about pacing: that if you do it right and choose your moments, you can go really pretty close to full tilt and still make it to the finish line. Full tilt is good.

The poet Edna St. Vincent Millay wrote the unofficial four-line anthem for us Type-A nut jobs:[9]

> *My candle burns at both ends;*
> *It will not last the night;*
> *But ah, my foes, and oh, my friends—*
> *It gives a lovely light!*

The great or at least prolific poet Anonymous boiled it down to five syllables:

> *Use it or lose it.*

Ms. Millay died when she was only 58,[10] but not from any sort of glorious flameout. She fell down the stairs in her house, which is so irrelevant to the tone of the poem that it's either useless filler or frighteningly poignant commentary on the arbitrary nature of it all. But *Use it or lose it* holds up better and better all the time.

Researchers touting the benefits of exercise in healthy, active individuals are vulnerable to accusations of gilding the lily,[11] but that doesn't seem to stop the papers from coming. And it's becoming clear that exercise helps even when you're not exactly on fire already. Active recovery has replaced idleness for the off days in training programs.[12] Evidence keeps mounting to show that the exercise that helps you recover from hard efforts also helps you recover from full-blown injuries[13] or worse. You can hardly read your first three get-well cards out of quadruple bypass surgery before the nursing staff is trying to get you to do laps around the med-surg unit. Meanwhile, we're not seeing so much new research extolling the health benefits of virtual hibernation that's not funded by mattress companies.

---

8   Not to mention solo ones, if you catch my drift.

9   Even for us obsessive-compulsive nut jobs who can't get past the fact that she screwed up the meter in the very first line.

10   Fifty-five to 59, rather.

11   Or what a professor friend of mine likes to call a "profound grasp of the obvious."

12   Major stage races like the Tour de France or the Giro d'Italia will throw a couple of rest days into the three weeks of racing. Standard procedure for these rest days is to go for about a 100 km bike ride.

13   So, when you torqued your ankle sliding into home in the Little League All-Star game and your dad's sympathy extended no further than "Walk it off," well, who knew?

That said, people do overdo it, and sometimes they flame out, burn out, or just drop out of the sport.[14]

All that scientific research can be accurate but still not 100 percent applicable. When the technical stuff gets too confusing, I find there can be just as much to be learned from the more mundane.[15] And in this case, I think about tires. Not spare tires—at least not the metaphorical kind. Bicycle tires.

Anyone who's done any serious shopping for performance tires has seen that the higher the performance of the tire, the faster the tire wears out. Call it the Edna St. Vincent Michelin equation. But there are three salient points here. The first: Sticky and supple and fragile or hard and bouncy and durable, they all wear out eventually. The second: Even the high-performance ones last a remarkably long time when you think about what you're putting them through.

The third: That's what tires are for.

---

14   More often than I care to consider, golf is involved. I hate golf. Last time some-
     one got me to play, I got in trouble for ricocheting a drive off the ball washer even
     though it wasn't my idea to put the ball washer there. That's not why I hate golf,
     but it hardly helps.

15   In fact, I think some college or university would do well to endow a professor-
     ship in the study of Mundanity. I would be all over that job. Any dean of any
     Department of Arts and Letters is welcome to contact me through VeloPress.
     You are holding my dissertation.

TALENTS

I don't own a racing team, but if I did, I would call it Team Fast Pig.

I would choose this name because of one of my favorite books by one of my favorite authors, and my favorite exchange in that book and possibly in all of literature. The book is John Steinbeck's *East of Eden*, and the exchange goes:

> [Adam said,] "You can't make a race horse out of a pig."
>
> "No," said Samuel, "but you can make a very fast pig."

Steinbeck was talking about humankind's eternal struggle between good and evil,[1] and I'm just talking about triathlons,[2] but the Samuel character and I seem to be on the same page about talent.

1　Actually, also in *East of Eden*, Steinbeck mentions that he doesn't believe there's even another theme out there worth writing about.

2　If Steinbeck is right (see note 1), this book is in peril. We get a few cheaters in this sport, and the occasional weenie, but in all these years I haven't seen much real evil.

Steinbeck keeps it simple and leaves the complicating and the obfuscating to the devoted readers and lesser writers. As a card-carrying member of both groups, I recognize that I'm more porcine than equine in the comparison he sets up, and I wonder if that doesn't put me on the better end of the deal. Steinbeck doesn't come out and say it, but something about the way he puts it gives me the impression that the horse has a destiny. The pig has a choice.

I am equal parts Welsh, German, Scottish, and Norwegian. Very Nordic. My ancestors bequeathed me a thick trunk, a long torso, short limbs, and a mass-to-skin ratio better suited to retaining heat than dissipating it.[3] In short (and stubby, ha!), I inherited a DNA code and heritage that predispose me toward sailing longboats past icebergs when I'd rather be good at combining three disparate types of long-distance self-propulsion.

And yet I can't thank my ancestors enough. If sailing, exploring, raiding, and pillaging[4] were their destined trades, I'm grateful they were programmed to be good at them. In such a line of work, one bad day at the office has serious implications in terms of surviving long enough to carry on the family name, and enough of my relatives got it right for long enough to plunk me down right here, right now, healthy if not gifted, in an era when I can write for money and race for a fee, and neither involves spending a lot of time on boats.

Think of that. I am fortunate to be alive during a very short window of human history[5] that happens to include triathlon[6] and just enough leisure to pursue it with some degree of seriousness. Talk about timing. It's unprecedented, really, to have it so good. It almost seems greedy to wish for more talent on top of it all.

Besides, if you're going to be a little short on talent, you could choose a worse sport than triathlon. With three times the normal quota of events, you've got three times the opportunity to hold your own. One of those opportunities is so technique-oriented that potbellied, septuagenarian

---

3   Though you'd think I'd reflect a little more of it. If my skin were any paler, I'd have to go into the haunting business.

4   And let us not forget avoiding the plague.

5   New York's Museum of Natural History has a spiraling, walk-through timeline representing the history of the universe. It's some 360 feet long; a normal footstep covers 75 million years. The part at the end, where humans exist, is as long as a single hair is thick. I'm no anthropologist, but I'm going to guess that if you were to take that hair's width of hominid history and stretch it into another 360-foot timeline, the part with time trial handlebars—hell, bicycles—would be even thinner.

6   Also, antibiotics that work. And my wife. Lyle Lovett. George Booth. Merino wool. Fig Newtons. And Steinbeck.

masters swimmers can lay waste to even the fittest triathlete. Another one makes use of a two-wheeled tool with gears and stuff[7] to even out any biomechanical hindrances, and the third, um, well, you can sure buy some brightly colored shoes and socks these days. Any one and all three will yield success and improvement for any athlete motivated enough to give it enough effort, time, study, sacrifice, pain, and bullheaded will.[8]

All of which makes those bastards who do have talent that much more infuriating. I confess to having noticed in myself feelings of jealousy toward squirrels. Not people who can't pedal in a straight line but actual squirrels! Where do they get off being able to outsprint me on legs that are two inches long? These feelings are assuaged effectively enough if I picture them trying to shop for a bicycle that fits, but if I'm jonesing for envy, the world is my oyster.[9]

It's bad enough that elite marathoners can run 26 miles at a faster pace than I can run 1, but do they have to do it at a lower heart rate than I hit while I'm tying my shoes? Professional cyclists are even worse, and it's my own fault for buying a power meter. Those guys use the same power meters, and their coaches or sponsors often publish charts and graphs of their speeds, their watts, and their corresponding heart rates for all to see. You can't help but try to compare, but putting your numbers up next to even a water-bottle-fetching *domestique*'s is like comparing your tax return to Microsoft's annual report. Some of the digits are recognizable, but the whole is an unfamiliar language.

Then again, I'm not sure I'd want the 2:10 marathoner's build come time to shovel snow out of the driveway.[10] Life is not a specialist's sport.

And let's remember that talent is a sliding scale. To paraphrase Abraham Lincoln, you can beat some of the people all of the time, and all of the people some of the time, but you cannot beat all of the people all of the time. And I'd tell him that even that much is generous, were he still alive and had he actually said it. No matter how good you are, somebody is better than you on any given day. In fact, very few people are so good that somebody's not better than them *every* given day.

To look at the sliding scale from another angle, sometimes *you're* the talented one. And you know what? Sometimes it's the greatest feeling, and sometimes it's a royal pain in the butt. In my tiny sphere of the local triathlon world, somehow I get pegged as the Guy Who Can Bike. Thus,

---

7   Sorry about the technical jargon.

8   Compare that to the old basketball recruiting adage, "You can coach technique, but you can't coach big."

9   In fact, I'm jealous of oysters, which can swim better than I can, or at least hold their breath longer.

10   I know: not a real issue in Kenya. Just indulge me while I make a larger point.

every other new friend I ride with seems to peg him- or herself as the One Who Doesn't Want to Look Bad in Front of the Guy Who Can Bike, and the first five miles or so—what riders my age prefer to call the Warm-up—are a hammerfest.

Races can offer a gentler perspective.

I remember finishing one particular triathlon happy enough with my race but certainly not feeling like the talented one. I was looking through the crowd of spectators for my wife and wandered over by the announcer's stand, where Charles Solomon[11] was rolling across the line on his bike with a whole run yet to go. "If Solomon can do it," the announcer cheerily told the crowd, "then so can you!"

My first thought was, "How about that? I'm glad I'm more talented than poor Charles Solomon." But he didn't seem embarrassed. He looked pretty pleased. I amended my thought: Compared to everyone who hadn't started the race, Charles Solomon was the talented one, and the gap between them and him was a lot more vast than the gap between him and me.

At the end of the day, we're all fast pigs.

Although, at the end of the story, may we all retire more like racehorses.

---

11   To pull a name out of the air.

CHAPTER 3

What We've Learned About Our Heads

GUTS

ncient physicians had a simple view of medicine. The body contained four humours: black bile, yellow bile, phlegm, and blood. These humours governed your health and your character. But Hippocrates and his peers were wrong. We now know that their view was twice as complex as it needed to be. What the body contains is guts. And there are only two[1] kinds:

1. Fear guts.[2]
2. Pain guts.[3]

Fear says, "You could die if you do this wrong." Pain says, "You will die if you keep this up."[4] To confront either head-on is to confront death. That's guts. And with all due respect to John Steinbeck and his assertion

---

1   No, I'm not including "beer guts." Do I *look* like a guy who just makes things up?
2   Fear guts are what send people into situations they know might hurt a lot. Fear guts are a popular form of guts for the same reasons the Ramones were a popular band. Everybody heard the Ramones and thought, "Well, hell, I can do that," even if they never got around to trying.
3   Pain guts are what keep people in situations that hurt when they could easily extricate themselves. Pain guts are more like listening to Joshua Bell play the violin. It's something to see, but doing it just sounds like too much work.
4   Maybe a better way of putting it is this: One form of guts is what gets you up the mountain before everyone else, and the other is what gets you back down it alive.

that the stalemate between good and evil is the only story worth telling, I think the struggle for courage is not only another story but maybe even the better one.

To do triathlon right demands and cultivates both kinds of guts. What risks to take? How hard to push? If a race is a scale model of life, it follows that the scary and the painful parts are concentrated versions of life's horrors as well.

No one in modern times has helped us face the Big Scary Painful Thing like Elisabeth Kübler-Ross. She wrote a book called *On Death and Dying*. The book's value[5] and its fame[6] are based on her outline of five distinct and dependable stages of grief. It is, in essence, a checklist for how people confront the end of the event. And I wonder if triathletes couldn't have come up with the same list of stages.[7]

Denial

A few years ago, I signed on for a commemorative[8] swim across the Straits of Mackinac, and that pissed off my mother-in-law. She had it in her head that swimming four miles[9] across a major shipping channel known for its unpredictable and rough conditions might be dangerous. Granted, my in-laws are not known for their derring-do,[10] but I could appreciate her concern. I couldn't agree with it, though. This was a well-planned, non-competitive event, and I was equipped and prepared and in the best shape of my life.[11] It would be the safest part of my summer, I assured her. Why, I regularly raced in deep[12] water with elbows and feet raining near-misses and direct blows at regions of my body that control vital functions like consciousness. I rode my bike and ran hundreds of miles a week on public roads with Michigan drivers[13] piloting heavy steel at high speeds within inches of me. I ran long distances in stupid hot and stupid cold weather on remote roads where help could be far away and passersby could be

---

5   Which, sure, still gets debated by people with advanced degrees; that's what people with advanced degrees do.

6   No one's debating that.

7   Triathletes couldn't have done it first, though, given that she wrote it in 1969—half a decade before people were racing their bikes around San Diego dripping seawater and fully 40 years before some presumptuous doofus had the nerve to suggest as much in his own book.

8   Happy fiftieth birthday, Mackinac Bridge.

9   Five by the time the current pushes you around.

10 I can't confirm this, but I think they have insurance policies on some of their insurance policies.

11 So far!

12 Deep enough.

13 I love my home state, but that's not a compliment.

scarce. So there. I don't know if my mother-in-law felt at all placated, but I had a whole new appreciation for my denial skills.[14]

Anger

I had done something wrong in the Deer Creek half-Ironman—biked too fast, eaten wrong, doesn't matter—and seized into a full-body cramp practically as I was coasting into the transition zone, and now I was midway through 13.1 miles of running like the Tin Man during his big rust scene in *The Wizard of Oz*. I was exuding pain guts, and I wasn't enjoying it. But I figured I'd make the most of it. One of the immutable truisms of writing is that there is no such thing as bad news; it's all potential material. So I commenced to writing, storing, and describing images in my

---

14 And yet my only truly scary bike crash happened when I was commuting on a balloon-tired rustmobile in the winter. I caught a wheel in a snow-covered crack, dumped quickly, and hit my head hard. I sat up and noticed that my vision was blurry in just one eye, and I couldn't imagine that that didn't portend something awful. I don't remember how long it took me to figure it out, but all it portended was that I'd knocked one lens out of my glasses.

head with the optimistic hope of future retrieval. The run route was two repetitions of an out-and-back course, so I crossed paths with everyone from the very fast to the people walking. I repeated a phrase to burn it into my brain: *"It looked like a triathlon had merged with a Volksmarch, and all that was missing was the yodeling."* I was still repeating it when I heard the music playing at the aid station just ahead. It was some hip-hop or rap mashup[15] of, I swear, *The Sound of Music*'s "High on a hill was a lonely goatherd, Lay ee odl lay ee odl lay hee hoo." Yodeling! I shook my fist at the gods as vigorously as my cramped arms allowed. It's one thing to ruin my race, but stealing my material is just plain wrong.

Bargaining

Triathlon has been a sport long enough that now some people just decide right from the start that they're going to be a triathlete. But when I started, most of us came to triathlon from a previous emphasis on[16] one of the three elements. I did, and my element was the bike. I fell into the trap of trying to survive the other two and make up the difference on the bike. What that approach got me was a regular place near the top of the results but never in the awards, a top bike split that impressed all of no one, and a guaranteed withering meltdown on the run. Eventually the throes were severe enough to induce Kübler-Rossian bargaining. I vowed to deemphasize my cycling and bring everything closer to the same level, to become a legitimate triathlete instead of a washed-up bike racer with a wetsuit. I'm not exactly sure which race prompted the epiphany, or, if you'd rather, apostasy,[17] but I know my high-pedigree triathlon bike was still fairly new and my race wheels[18] were brand-new, so it took some pretty serious melting down to forge a deal like that. Now. Crisis-based bargains tend to evaporate faster than sweat in Santa Fe once the crisis passes. I half expected my newfound program of excellence through entropy to dry up the same way, but instead I had a breakthrough season. The temptation to hammer is still there, so maybe it's just that the crisis hasn't passed. Or maybe it's just that I'm not getting passed as much.

Depression

I was 24. My dad was 50. He had talked me into an attempt at the father-son division of the Michigan National 24-Hour Challenge bicycle event.

---

15 Gwen Stefani's "Wind It Up," it turned out.

16 If not proficiency in.

17 Take your pick. Use either in pretentious conversation. Use only the former in job interviews.

18 Which shouldn't even be written into a paragraph with "bargain" in it.

It was dark and cold and wet, and I was depressed. I had come into it fit enough, racing criteriums every weekend and the rare road race, but this long, slow, overnight nonsense was new. I had done all right for the first 250 miles, easily hanging with the small pack of leaders, but I had lost them when they'd lied about a truce to answer nature's call.[19] Now it was pushing midnight, I was hypothermic,[20] and quitting seemed like as reasonable an option as it ever had. The father-son title was not only improbable, it was unappealing. Only one thing was going to get me out of my funk, and that was more depression, compliments of my dad. He was still behind me. Way behind me, to be sure; moving slowly but moving nonetheless; and close enough that if I quit and he kept tweedling along, he would finish with more miles than I and I'd be even more depressed long after I stopped shivering. He did keep tweedling along, but so did I. He won his age group, I won mine, and we not only won the father-son title but broke the record. And I was still depressed. "This," I thought, "is not what I was hoping to be good at."

Acceptance

Sometimes the wind is just going to be in your face, figuratively or literally, and there's nothing you can do but make friends with it. Dick and I were backpacking in Montana's Beartooth Range, sitting on a ledge way above treeline while a storm blew straight into our faces at a good 50 mph. It was cold and uncomfortable and probably a bad idea to be up there. Dick, as it happened, was a world authority on Third World economics and no stranger to adverse conditions. He leaned over and ripped a thunderous fart. "I'd apologize," he said, "but it's already a quarter mile behind us."[21]

Yeah. Maybe we're experts in risk, too.

Wouldn't bet my life on it, though.

---

19   Or maybe their idea of a short truce didn't allow for a major transaction in the portable jakes halfway up the long park driveway. Not that I could blame them. Or myself.

20   Turns out I was as stupid to believe the weather forecast as I was to believe the nature's-call-truce guys.

21   Yeah, I've got a friend who's a world-class economist. I've got friends who are elite athletes, and I've got friends who are elite comedians, assuming there is such a thing. The economist may not do triathlons, and the athletes may not know GDP from DNF, but everyone loves a fart joke.

DETERMINATION

W illiam Shakespeare famously wondered, "What's in a name?" I will suggest, much less famously, that a whole lot is in a name.[1] One reason I love being from Michigan is that it's the home of a sports car rally named the Press-on-Regardless. I'm not a car guy, so I really don't know much about the rally,[2] but I love that name.[3]

Press on regardless.

Isn't that what we do, as humans and as athletes? Press on? It is. Regardless is how we do it. As humans, we press on because we must. As

---

[1] Put it this way: The line goes, "What's in a name? That which we call a rose by any other name would smell as sweet." It's from *Romeo and Juliet*. What if Shakespeare had named the play *Stinky Otis and Heifer-Haunches Henderson*? He'd have been back to waiting tables, that's what.

[2] Except that in 1951, the winning car was an MG TC, which race records say was driven by "Mr. Preston" with his navigator "Mrs. Preston"; that evokes the kind of image that could get even me a little interested in cars.

[3] Don't like the hyphens, though. It makes it sound less like a road rally than a brand of false fingernails, but we'll let that slide.

athletes, we press on to discover that we can. As triathletes, we press on because we deliberately make sure we have to.

And it all ties together. If you had to pare endurance down to its essence, it could probably be expressed quite nicely as a simple ratio of effort over time. And like most simple answers, it's right on the money and not even close.

Effort? What's that? Sometimes it's pushing hard. Sometimes it's holding back. Maybe it hurts, and maybe it doesn't. Maybe it hurts me, but the same effort doesn't hurt someone else so much.[4] Maybe it hurts one year, one day, while on another day the same effort feels like nothing. Effort during a race comes off differently than effort during training— oddly, the more so the more you train.

Time? What's *that?* We race for hours to obsess over minutes and seconds, and then we look back on each race as its own individual moment. No matter the distance, no matter the result, each race begins at the starting line and ends at the finish line. The minutes and seconds just give it shape, which makes room for more moments. Nobody says, "Yes, I experienced a sensation of discomfort at perhaps a level 8 on a scale of 1 to 10 for a period of 2 minutes, 11 seconds. . . ." No. They say, "Man, that hill sucked."

If a race is a moment made of moments, then maybe a whole season is but a moment as well. Maybe a lifetime is. It makes you wonder about that business of people watching their lives flash before their eyes in the seconds before they check out. Are they seeing an ultracondensed replay? Or is that all the longer the whole show lasted?

I'm not trying to get off on some kind of far-flung, mystic tangent,[5] but the whole concept of life-as-a-moment does change the way I look at things. When I'm in the middle of a half hour of agony, just imagine the relief I feel knowing that it's really only lasting a moment. Or the relief I *will* feel when the concept finally sinks in to the point where I can believe it. I'm sure it will happen. Eventually. I keep telling myself it will only . . . be . . . a moment.

---

4   Often it hurts me because I'm trying to convince someone else it doesn't. See if this doesn't sound familiar: I'll bury myself to catch up to someone, and when I get there I breathe slowly, maybe carry on a little small talk, go into oxygen debt all over again to make it *(please, God)* look like *(please God, please)* I'm feeling good enough that it would be folly to counterattack. Of course, the folly is mine. Anyone I want to intimidate is going to see right past the breathing to my soaked clothing, my salt-crusted skin, and the fact that it took me a while to get there. Yet somehow the people with less competitive intentions interpret my ruse as, *Oh, Jef is feeling good; I should probably pick up the pace so I don't slow him down.*

5   No time for that!

At the very least, every moment of suffering you experience is a moment of suffering you survive,[6] and every moment you survive is one you can compare to the ordeal at hand. Every triathlete has his or her go-to low point, the day that makes everything pale—or, rather, glow—in comparison. I'm sure Tim DeBoom remembers Ironman Kona 2003, where, well into the run, he was looking like a lock for his third consecutive world championship until he passed a kidney stone.[7] I have a friend, a scary good trail runner from the West Coast,[8] who headed out for a big race, realized it was October 31, and worried that he would look like a killjoy if he didn't run in a Halloween costume. He improvised. He rushed home, found a frilly pink-and-black cocktail dress,[9] put it on, and headed back to the race . . . where he was the only one with a costume.[10]

My go-to bad day is not so dramatic. It's a bike ride to visit my parents at their house 70 miles away, when the weather started out with 50 degrees and a strong tailwind,[11] then segued to a soaking rain en route to a 90-degree shift in the wind direction and a 40-degree drop in temperature. That one has some staying power, but it's getting old.[12] I'm sure it's due to be replaced.[13] You know I'll be out there trying.

Every effort is an opportunity. An opportunity for a bad day, for a good day, for improvement, for a story. I've collected a few of those stories, and it's easy to notice that they don't all take place during a race. Indeed, I used to wonder if racing wasn't just an excuse to train. It's not a bad plan. Training like that not only takes effort, it takes a certain amount of self-centeredness that the rest of the world has trouble reconciling with what it thinks you owe it. There was a time when I didn't train to race so much as I raced to train. But I've since come to believe that it's all one and the same. Racing is a fine excuse, but it's a better goal. And it's more than that.

---

6   And at the very most, every moment but one.

7   !

8   A detail probably worth keeping in mind.

9   I didn't ask, and you wouldn't have, either.

10   He won the race, too. His strategy was to let a few rabbits go during the first half of the race, then chase them down during the second half. His strategy apparently did not include looking at the race information too closely, so in addition to running through the scrub in a frilly dress, he was chasing ghosts. Concurrent with the half-marathon was a quarter-marathon, and his rabbits had veered off to find their own finish line. When he finished chasing, he had broken the course record by 4 minutes. He didn't stick around for the awards ceremony. He didn't have anything nice to wear.

11   Let me be the first to use the word "tailgale."

12   Pretty obvious it took place before you could just look up a weather map online.

13   Oh, boy!

The race is what makes it triathlon instead of exercise.

At some point during the race, if you're doing it right, you reach a point where things start to get dicey, and success—whatever success is to you—comes down to determination. You find a way. A way to finish, a way to win, a way to cross the line anonymously in the middle of the pack knowing that "I did my best" was a promise fulfilled and not an excuse proffered.

I'd like to say you remember how you got through so you can do it the next time, but that isn't my experience. You're a little foggy when it happens. It fails to make sense outside the original context.[14] It changes from race to race, anyway. Mostly you just remember that you *did* find a way,

---

14   That is, "I guess you had to be there."

that you can, and that seems to be enough. And if it's enough to get you through the next race, it's enough to get you *to* the next race in a world that's often supportive but reliably indifferent and inherently selfish and occasionally mean.

Robert Frost wrote what might be my favorite poem, what most certainly *is* my favorite poem if you ask me on the right day. It goes:

> *Forgive, O Lord, my little jokes on thee,*
> *And I'll forgive thy great big one on me.*

I originally liked it because there were times when I really did feel like the butt of a big cosmic joke.[15] Then I liked it because I thought maybe I, too, could forgive it all. But it turns out that I like it for an even better reason. Now I've had a few years and a lot of races to test my limits, learn from mistakes, lose my confidence, gain some insight, see some of the world, laugh at my humanness, and pee in my wetsuit. And sometimes, just once in a while, I can almost convince myself I'm in on the gag.

Press-on-Regardless.

That could be the name of any and every triathlon, but we'll leave it to the auto racers. Because even though there's enough room between our starting line and our finish line for something like a whole life, it somehow seems too claustrophobic for the credo.

15 Who hasn't?

APPETITE

For all the good things triathlon does for my body, it does even more for my head. I'm sure there are all sorts of chemical and sociological reasons for this, but, as much as anything, all that time spent training makes it impossible to watch very much television.

Not that TV programming is predominantly crap. It is, but so what? Sturgeon's Law[1]—90 percent of everything is crap[2]—reminds us that

---

1   Here's how it supposedly goes down: Theodore Sturgeon was an influential science fiction author in the mid–twentieth century. When some master of diplomacy mentioned to him that 90 percent of science fiction was crap, Sturgeon replied that, well, 90 percent of *everything* was crap. (Oddly, Sturgeon himself insisted that that was not Sturgeon's Law, but it didn't turn out that it was his call to make. Even the *Oxford English Dictionary* says Sturgeon's Law is the 90-percent-crap one. But Sturgeon said that was Sturgeon's *Revelation* because there was already a Sturgeon's *Law*, which, in about as tight a literal symmetry as you can get when throwing around the word "crap," goes, "Nothing is always absolutely so."

2   You know what? I bet Sturgeon and his friend didn't settle for the word "crap," either.

television hardly has the corner on that. But it's especially nice to avoid the commercials and the sportscasters. Ninety percent of which are, of course, yeah.

The commercials, what you have to worry about is the other 10 percent because they are so incredibly good at their purpose, which is to make you feel like your life is gloomy and depressing and can be salvaged only by purchasing whatever it is they're pitching in that 30 seconds. With the sportscasters, on the other hand, 90 percent seems conservative anytime you hear one of them wrap up a complicated contest that could and did hinge on any of an infinite combination of complex and subtle factors, saying that it simply came down to "who wanted it more."[3]

Who *wanted* it more? Since when does anything in this multifarious world boil down to something as simple as desire?

Okay. It happens all the time. Desire is not so simple[4] after all. It may be the least simple thing there is if complexity of consequence is any measure.[5]

Like, why would anybody want to do something as time-consuming and expensive and uncomfortable and painful and even risky as a triathlon? Where does that desire come from? Appetite is a strange and elusive concept. Anyone who's had the flu[6] knows that when you have an appetite, you can't understand people who don't, and when you don't have one, you can't relate to the people who do.

Triathletes' motivations are as unique as snowflakes in the Yukon, at that latitude where some of them melt away and most last just about forever but get blown all over the place so they're tough to keep track of. I know my motives vary from race to workout to diet to spreadsheet,[7] some of which my friends and adversaries and I share and some of which we don't.

You've been reading about my motives in this book.[8] Everyone else in the field, in the sport, races for the same reasons and for completely different ones. There are people who do it because they've got something to prove, including a lucky subset who actually know what it is they're proving. Some people race because they love their spouses; some race to

---

3　Leaving me to wonder what kind of analysis he might come up with if he wanted to do his job a little more.

4　Which only firms up my stance on those sportscasters, because they're pretending it *is* simple.

5　Note the Samson and Delilah story. Or *The Iliad*. Or the Clinton presidency.

6　Or worse; strength to all of you.

7　And recovery. I swear, if I could just figure out how to motivate myself to get enough sleep, I might be dangerous.

8　One of them *is* this book, come to that.

get away from their spouses.[9] Some race to raise money for a cause or a living for themselves. Some race simply because they're good at it;[10] some because they're not sure they'll ever be as good at something else.[11] To lose weight. To gain fitness. To recapture youth, to forestall age. Certain professionals who don't get out enough[12] need to race and train with other people; others[13] see maybe a little too much of other people and relish the chance to train alone. Some, at some point, got into it because they didn't know any better and now can't find a way out.[14] And everybody, at one point or another, races to justify some piece of equipment they bought.

I don't believe any one person races for any single reason, nor does anyone's motivational matrix match the next one's, nor even his or her own a day later. But there are a few common threads at the more important seams, none so strong as pure force of habit. I've been doing this so long I can't imagine not doing it, and when my other motives fail me,[15] that's the cable that holds it together.

So imagine how impressed I am by people who don't yet have that reserve chute. I help out with the Hawk Island Triathlon where I live in mid-Michigan. It's a sprint, and while we'll accommodate experienced sandbaggers,[16] the emphasis is on welcoming newcomers to the sport.[17] Man, those guys impress me. I cannot remember or imagine what gets them there, and I remember and imagine things for a living.

But once in a while I get a peek. As I type this, the Hawk-I-Tri is just one day away, and this edition's field of rookies includes my wife and my mother. Patty has multiple sclerosis. Mom is about to turn 72. Patty's nerves are scarred. Mom's bones are porous. Patty has lost a little lean flesh over the years. Mom has gained some flesh. Patty cannot run. Mom cannot run. Patty and Mom will not be stopped.

Where the hell did that come from? What made them want it? Both of them have been watching me do this stuff for years, but the connection is not so direct. We'll rewind. Patty, Mom, granddaughter, brother. Stop. Play.

---

9   These two are not even close to mutually exclusive.
10 I always wondered: Is this where certain other professions come from? Somebody aces the proctology unit in med school, and boom, there they are?
11 I don't wonder for a moment if this is where writers and cartoonists come from.
12 Back to writers already.
13 Police officers, therapists, anybody with a boss.
14 Remember this from earlier: Ignorance + Desperation? I still cannot oversell this formula for success.
15 And they do. And I promise you they will. No one loves this sport more than I do, and it happens.
16 Like me, if I were fast enough.
17 A gateway substance, as it were.

My mother's grandson, Patty's and my nephew, was screwing up. He was 15 and figuring out that he was no longer 10 and that the world was now less interested in what it could do for him than it was in what he could do for it, and he was finding brooding lassitude to be a satisfactory response. But he seemed to like how things worked out for his uncle and expressed something that looked at the time like interest, maybe even enthusiasm. His mother was a decent runner, and her husband was a solid swimmer. I gave him my spare road bike for the summer and a whole bunch of gear for(apparently)ever, and he and his family signed up for a triathlon relay.[18] He trained very little,[19] finished his race on guts and youth,[20] and promptly returned to his shell. But his younger sister was watching. She wanted in on the action and signed up for the same race the next year. She was 11 and had no business in a race of that difficulty.[21] She finished[22] last overall and first in her age group.

My mother had been watching over the years, too, and found a way into the same race. This triathlon had a 5K run–only option. She was there with her 2-year-old twin grandkids, and she bought a number and pinned it on, and when the triathletes started swimming, she started walking, pushing the double-wide stroller up and down the hills and over the asphalt and gravel. My mother would never seek to be the center of attention, but she'd found it by accident and it seemed to suit her. The run course doubled back on itself a few times, and when I passed her and high-fived her and told her she was awesome, I all but had to wait in line each time. She won her age group, too. We all found a restaurant and had lunch before we split up and headed to our homes. I think that was where she first asked if they let you walk in a whole triathlon, too.

When I started helping Mom work up a training plan, Patty was looking over my shoulder. The idea that you could walk in a triathlon was not news to her. She'd seen it. That her mother-in-law was nuts[23] was no revelation, either, nor was the underlying theme of Patty's own competitive streak. Inside that triangle of old news was new inspiration, and just like that, I was filling out training plans and race registrations for all three of us.

Of the three of us, I've been sticking to my training plan the worst. It's been one of those years when work can be overwhelming,[24] and even

---

18   Putting the lie to that bit about the world's lack of interest in his well-being.
19   Ignorance.
20   Desperation.
21   Ignorance.
22   Desperation.
23   And wonderfully so.
24   I'm writing a book!

with a normal allotment of leisure time, there's not always enough for both first-time coaching and self-centered training. While Patty and Mom are out there struggling Sunday, I'll be hurting, too, and it's not going to bring me a personal record as it will them.

This is about as much of a shock as my wife's competitiveness and my mom's exquisite insanity. I'll confess that I've spent the whole spring girding myself for the dreaded Bad Day, when the double whammy of frustration and discouragement destroys my appetite like coliform bacteria in the coleslaw. I've still got a day to go, but it hasn't happened.

I'm learning one more thing about desire.

If there's anything as satisfying as feeding your own appetites, it's cooking for others.

Bon appétit.

EPILOGUE

PATTY AND MOM both finished the Hawk Island Triathlon. Patty was 641st. Mom, 642nd. Out of 642 finishers. Out of 700 entrants. Out of 10 million Michiganders. Out of 300 million Americans.

Out of the *Didn't*s and into the *Did*s.

It took a while. There was suffering. There was staggering.

It wasn't pretty, but it was beautiful.

APPENDIX
by Patty Mallett

IF YOU'RE A TRIATHLETE, this section's not for you—to put it in racing terms, you've already crossed the finish line. This section is for your spouse, your significant other, your friend, or your coworker who has found him- or herself in a ménage à trois of sorts with you and your sport of choice.

If you're not a triathlete, you're probably reading this book because you're involved—in some way or another—with one. Maybe you married a triathlete. Or you're dating one, or you're friends with one, or you work with one.[1] And you want to be supportive of (or at least polite about) his or her, um, obsession.

Welcome. This section is for you.

Trust that I speak from experience. Jef has competed in at least 50 triathlons in the 21 years of our marriage, and I've probably attended two-thirds of them as his personal cheering section. (I even got around to competing in one myself!)

I've watched mysterious powders take over counter space in our kitchen and listened as Jef referred—in all seriousness—to the bars of compressed whatever and packets of gels in his pockets as "food." I've done my best to understand lengthy conversations about things like "mean maximal power" and "lactate threshold"—conversations that take place with very little actual input from me. I've written checks for major triathlon-related purchases.[2]

---

1   Or maybe you married/are dating/are friends with/work with a once perfectly normal human being who has since turned into a triathlete. It happens.

2   If you're married to or seriously involved with a triathlete, listening politely while ongoing equipment needs are discussed can get complicated, especially if your finances are intertwined. If your triathlete is at all like mine, the equipment needs will start small—a swim cap here, a pair of running shoes there—then grow as interest in the sport grows. Before long, you'll find yourself discussing, in all seriousness, the purchase of a tri-specific bicycle that costs more than your monthly mortgage payment. My advice here? Assuming you're not having problems making your monthly mortgage payment, and assuming your triathlete is actually using the previous purchases, *give in and buy the bike.* You'll be repaid in spades with a happy, healthy spouse/significant other who, not coincidentally, has a really cute butt from all the bicycling.

If you do all of these things, you'll be your triathlete's hero. But watching a triathlon is the best way to show your support, and it's way more fun than listening to endless talk about "average wattage" and "aero bars."[3] While triathlon's not a particularly spectator-friendly sport—there's no neat rectangular playing field on which all the action takes place while you sit in the stands with a hot dog and a box of popcorn—it's not unfriendly, either. You just need to know what to expect.

I can help. Here's what to expect—divided into three parts in keeping with the triathlon theme.

Early start times: Even a sprint triathlon requires 5 kilometers (3.1 miles) of running and 20 kilometers (12.4 miles) of cycling on public roads, and local officials are generally more willing to block off intersections and disrupt traffic early in the day, when traffic volume is light. Triathlons are usually well under way by 8 a.m.

If you're going to the triathlon with your triathlete, you can expect an even earlier start to allow time to pick up the race packet, get body markings, meticulously lay out the race gear in the transition area, and warm up. Most triathletes are unlikely to appreciate assistance with any of these tasks.

Bring a chair (the nylon kind that folds up so you can stuff it into a bag and haul it around easily is great for triathlons), a bottle of water, a cup of coffee, and a newspaper or magazine.[4] Bring a few snacks for yourself, too, especially if the triathlon is any longer than a sprint. Your breakfast will wear off before you know it, and it's impolite to nosh on the stuff that's there to feed the athletes. Find a place to land within sight of your triathlete's spot in the transition area (but outside it—race officials generally don't want anyone in the transition area but triathletes and volunteers), and get comfortable. You're going to be there a while. Relax and enjoy it.

Lots of downtime: One of the best ways to watch a triathlete compete is to stay within sight of the transition area. You can count on a reappearance between the swim and the bike and between the bike and the run.

I like to watch Jef start his swim, then go back to my chair outside the transition area and read my *Detroit Free Press* or *People* magazine[5] until he reappears, dripping, in transition to get on his bike. (I've tried to watch him in the water, but it's pointless—one hundred people in wetsuits and

---

3   Aero bars are not, in fact, edible, although they may not differ markedly in substance from your triathlete's favorite "food."

4   Books require a bit too much attention during the race, and they're tougher to stuff into the bag with the chair after the race.

5   A guilty pleasure reserved for airports and triathlons.

yellow[6] swim caps all tend to look alike. Besides, he's swimming. He can't see or hear me cheering him on. I may as well trust that he'll make it safely back to shore and spend my next half hour getting caught up on celebrity news.[7])

Once Jef heads off on his bicycle, I can settle back into my chair and read until he's due to show up in transition again. I cheer wildly while he puts on his running shoes and leaves, then sit back and wait for him to finish the race.

This is where it comes in handy to watch the same triathlete regularly, especially if his or her finish times are at all consistent. Jef's schedule for an Olympic-distance triathlon is wonderfully predictable. If his swim wave takes off at 8 a.m., I'll see him in transition by 8:30. He'll be back again after the bike leg a little after 9:30 a.m. and finished with the entire race by 10:30 or so.

A good time: It's hard not to have fun at a triathlon, especially if you're not doing all the hard work. If you're a people watcher, you'll enjoy the wide array of humanity taking part in the race—first-timers working toward bragging rights, experienced triathletes putting another notch in their fuel belts, fat people, thin people, old people, young people.[8] Give them each a round of applause as they go by, would you?

One of my all-time favorite triathlons (one that, alas, no longer exists) had a run course that went past my aunt and uncle's house. I'd see Jef off on the swim and head to their house, where we'd set up lawn chairs in the driveway, drink coffee, eat doughnuts,[9] and cheer wildly for every person who went by. I saved my loudest cheers for the people who looked like they needed it the most[10]—especially the last of the finishers.

Was I obnoxious? Probably. But I was also right. When I finally competed[11] in a triathlon of my own, I learned how much it meant to have

---

6   Or whatever Day-Glo color they happen to assign to your triathlete's wave.
7   Did you know Matt Damon, Jennifer Lopez, and Matthew McConaughey have all done triathlons? So has Lance Armstrong, but he doesn't really count—he started his professional athletic career as a triathlete before figuring out that bicycling was his best event.
8   I love the triathlons in which the race organizers deem it necessary to put the triathletes' ages on their legs. What better proof that the sport is a fountain of youth? Here comes a woman with cuts I can envy—and she's 15 years older than I am! Here comes a guy with legs that inspire lustful thoughts—and he's 20 years older!
9   A serious guilty pleasure when you're watching a triathlon.
10 And Jef. Duh.
11 "Raced" doesn't seem like quite the right word for someone who finished second-to-last (ahead of only my 72-year-old mother-in-law, who won her age group) in her only triathlon, a "sprint" that ultimately took her almost four hours to finish. "Triathlete" does, though.

someone cheering you on—even if it was someone you'd never seen before and would probably never see again. I was exceedingly grateful for the kindness of strangers and irritated in equal measures by the doofus on the bike course who told me to "hurry up" because I was "way behind."

When I finally staggered across the finish line—3:47:52 after starting—there was a noisy group of family and race volunteers greeting my arrival. I felt like a rock star.[12] I felt like a triathlete.

Don't be stingy with your cheers. Hug your sweaty triathlete[13] at the finish line. It's a big accomplishment.

And you helped make it happen.

---

12   A very tired, spent rock star. Keith Richards, perhaps.
13   Wear something machine-washable.

ACKNOWLEDGMENTS

THE STUPIDEST RULE IN TRIATHLON has to be the one that says, "No outside assistance."

Nobody does a triathlon solo. It takes too much support, patience, teaching, experience, indulgence, shared rides, group workouts, and hand-me-down stuff from too many people to even think about calling triathlon an individual sport. I could write a whole book thanking everyone who has helped me, and I kinda sorta just did.

Nobody writes a book solo, either, and I sure didn't.

I can't name everyone I owe, but there are a few who need to go on the record:

MY WIFE, Patty Mallett, whose life is inconvenienced by all this training and racing and writing as surely as my own is; who encourages it outwardly even those times when she's just putting up with it inwardly; who, to better understand it all, went and tried it herself.

MY PARENTS, Gordon and Janet Mallett, who taught me that writing and drawing was a fine way to work and that sweating and failing and trying again was a fine way to play; for a lifetime (so far!) of encouragement, support, and unabashed fandom; for solid enough genes to be a passable amateur but not a stressed-out pro.

LEGIONS OF TRAINING PARTNERS AND FRIENDS, but none more than Brian Bess, who over the years has heard every story in this book a dozen times, knows he'll hear them again, and still trains with me.

MORE FRIENDS who read the book as I was writing it and offered feedback, questions, reassurance, and the right words at the right time. But none more than Al Bliss, who may have spent more time reviewing it than I spent writing it.

THE PROFESSIONALS—who also have become friends—at VeloPress, who saw to it that my writing makes my enthusiasm more understandable, not less so. And none more than Renee Jardine, who got it in her head that I might write something informative, enlightening, entertaining, and on time—and nobly settled for most of those.

PEOPLE EVERYWHERE who work for their fun; people who get it.

ABOUT THE AUTHOR AND ILLUSTRATOR

JEF MALLETT is the creator of the award-winning comic strip *Frazz*, syndicated by United Feature Syndicate. He illustrated the award-winning bicycle racing book *Roadie*.

David Trumpie, Trumpie Photography

He has lived in Michigan all his life; he still lives there with his wife and spends altogether too much time tripping over four cats, one dog, countless retired running shoes, and the best-laid schemes of mice and men.

Jef raced his first triathlon in 1981 and never looked back, though he has a tendency to look off to the side an awful lot. He's raced every standard distance from sprint to Ironman—never won the whole thing and never bailed out of one. He's not about to quit entering triathlons, either, so look for him at your next race. You just never know.